On Being God

Beyond Your Life's Purpose

Carl Bozeman

Copyright owner website: http://www.onbeinggod.com

ISBN: 1-4392-4484-7
ISBN-13: 9781439244845

Visit www.booksurge.com to order additional copies.

Table of Contents

Introduction

The things I used to consider unique and exclusive of just me, my history, are no longer important in either identifying myself or giving context to any part of my present life. Many parts of my life were very dark and I learned to identify with the part of myself that suffered and would tell *my story* as a means to shock my listeners or to manipulate family and friends into providing me a certain amount of attention at the telling. It is common to do this as many of us have histories we identify ourselves with. The events and circumstances that formed and shaped my identity no longer hold me in its chains. I have since come to know that the past does not exist except in the minds of those who choose to pull it into the present which most of us do anyway.

While most of us think that we are a culmination of all the events, actions, and circumstances of past experience, we are not. Who we are exists outside anything we have done in the past or hope to do in the future. We are eternal beings who are a part of an earthly *now* that is only one possibility in an infinite number of possibilities. We are, in fact, travelers who exist outside any dimension of time or space who stopped by Earth for a visit. We should relish the experience in every way our senses will allow us. We are infinite, made up of all that is, and we will always be so. We are not here for any grand purpose or to learn lessons of a divine nature or to prepare for future earthly engagements. We are, simply, *here!* While it seems we are locked in a three- dimensional reality to which we are forever confined, it is only because we have so fully accepted that there is nothing else and that we are bound to the laws that serve this reality. Being constrained by such laws puts us in the realm of being ruled by them. It is only so because *we* accept it to be true. Most of us are conditioned over the course of our lives to think and believe as we do. We are taught, relentlessly, to accept what our conditioning tells us is important and in the process of that conditioning, our eyes are closed to truth that is so profound and wondrous most of us would shrink before such knowing.

Outside of what we think we know about ourselves is only the tip of a huge iceberg, and we cannot neither see nor comprehend it. In a way, we all seem to intuit within us something far greater than what or who we believe we are, but when we explore such possibilities the noise of our minds, the culmination of our histories, experiences, and education, casts a dark shadow over us. In other words, we are literally talked out of what or who we truly are by the chatter of our own minds. Our real identity is buried in the noise of our reason and debate. We accept this noise and debate, identify ourselves with it, and lose our true selves to it. We are not what we think nor are we the past from whence we came or the future where we direct ourselves. All that exists, hence all that we are, exists right now and *only* now! We do not exist in the future nor are we victims of any past experience. There is only now and it is neither good nor bad. *Now* simply is and it is the only place of power any of us have. Most of us give away the power of our *present time* to our past or to our hopes for the future. Such power, if harnessed right now without the weight of historical suffering or dreams of a better day in the future, would open our eyes to not only the huge iceberg beneath the tip we see, but the entire ocean in which it all resides. Our greatness exceeds any metaphor. We are boundless!

For me this knowing came suddenly and in such an unexpected way it may sound simplistic or farfetched. While I have always been a searcher, like most, I was looking for answers that made sense in the time-space reality we live in. I was looking for a magic bullet, a fully explainable formula for all of life's greatest mysteries. Like all searchers, I read everything I thought would steer me to a comprehensible answer. My search took me into disciplines of science, physics, philosophy, metaphysics, self help, religion, and so much more but answers that met my criteria for being believable were slow in coming. In fact, they didn't come at all to my satisfaction. I never gave up but I often questioned whether such things could ever be known, let alone understood. What came to me is exactly the opposite of anything I expected or had previously determined would constitute an answer that would leave me without question or doubt.

On December 6, 2005 I was visiting three of my children in California. As we always do, we spent time visiting, dining out and going to movies and any number of other things we can squeeze into my visits with them. On that night we had had a late dinner but decided to go to a movie that would not be starting for about an hour and a half. While we waited, my daughter Jana brought out a DVD of the movie "The Secret" which I had never heard of. She compared it to the movie "What the Bleep do We Know" which I had seen so we all agreed to sit and watch while killing some time before having to leave for the movie. I could not stop watching. In fact, going to the movies never came up again as we all watched "The Secret" unfold. I was shaken to my core and pressed upon so powerfully with an awareness, insight, and comprehension that to this day remains inexplicable. With the exception of Denis Waitley and Jack Canfield, I had never heard of any of the other teachers in the movie. I was particularly taken in by Esther Hicks and couldn't believe that I had never heard of the "Teachings of Abraham" she had supposedly authored. Later I realized she was a channel and that the teachings were not about the biblical Abraham as I thought they were. Who were these people and how was it possible that in all the reading I had done over so many years I had not come upon them?

Equally perplexing about the way this came to me is that in the growing awareness sweeping over me, I recognized that I had always known these truths but I also knew so much more. Not just about the Law of Attraction as taught in "The Secret" but the infinite and divine nature of man and that what we see and believe in this reality is such a small part of what and who we are. How could it be that I somehow knew this all along? It was as if all the cells of my body suddenly woke up and made every part of me buzz with awareness. That's all I can say about it. I was overwhelmed. All the reading, pondering, and searching for answers in the contexts of religion, science, and philosophy came into sharp focus for me, a clarity that I knew I had always known. I know it sounds funny but it was like waking up from an amnesiac state with the full recall of everything previously lost. Sudden and profound, it was all there— a knowing at a cellular, if not a quantum level. I could not stop the waves of pulsating, vibrating energy that poured over me. I was simply swept up in something wonderful that to this day I find difficult to explain.

Something else occurred while I was caught up in this state of knowing that I will share as well. I was aroused to an *awakening* that is permeating all peoples, places, and indeed, all things on earth. Some term it 'enlightenment' while others call it 'Christ Consciousness' but whatever it is called, millions around the world are beginning to hear the inner voice *we all know* but rarely comprehend. As I felt the warm buzz of energy sweeping over me, I knew that I was a part of this awakening and that I would be a vehicle through whom others would come to a similar awareness. As I watched the movie, the words kept pouring through my mind that "I am a part of this." I knew that I was not only being awakened to this new awareness but that I was being called to it. I have felt this at times throughout my life but never before had I heard the call as clearly as on this night. It is exciting to be among those who have heard a familiar voice and are waking up to that which is great and incredible in us.

I should point out that this is not a book about the Law of Attraction. While I know that we attract to us those things our thoughts and feelings focus on this book identifies our true nature in the universe. I know the words I have written will ring true for many and awaken many more to this new energy that is rising in the hearts and minds of people all over the world.

I might also add that what I have written I have little or no recall of having written it. I did not hear a voice and dictate as has been the experience of some. I simply held pen in hand and the words manifested on paper before me. I'm not sure where they came from or who guided my hand. Throughout my life I have been aware of what I term *other realities*. I have always seen things that made me wonder if I was possessed by something evil and while I puzzled over these glimpses into other awarenesses I could never find an explanation for them. The circumstances, education both academic and religious, events and conditioning of my life always had me questioning these odd powers I have. They even became scary to me and I avoided situations in which they could be called to bear. To me it was *voodoo* and I wanted no part of it and struggled to keep it at bay. Since that night in December, 2005 I am no longer afraid and have come to understand that what I once was afraid of should be developed and used for some greater good. I am humbled by this force that has worked through me in the writing of this book and showing me a greater awareness of all that is. I call it "My Father" or "God."

This is a message to individuals. The divine is within each of us, not in institutions, governments, nations, places, or things. What is written here must speak to the hearts and souls of those individuals who seek it or it does not speak at all. It matters not either way. Some will hear it and receive it while others will not. It is all good. We all know the words of Gandhi that "We must be the change we seek." Change does not occur through us; it happens *because* of us. Jesus explained that the "Kingdom of God is within each of us" but it is the individual, the "I Am," that must find that kingdom and as we find it and change, so too will our world.

The voice of God tells us that we are far greater than anything we can conceive of and that there is so much more to our existence than what we perceive through our three-dimensional form. The mind, however, cannot translate what the voice of God tells us so the mind fights against the voice with reason and scientific or religious support. The voice of God is our own voice but it is not the chattering that runs incessantly in our minds. The chattering voice must be silenced and in such quiet, the voice of the divine will be heard. We are *the* divine! Everything in our reality whether it be our beliefs, fantasies, ideas, deities, whatever is all part of a construct, is the creation of our very active and analytical minds. The mind constructs this so-called reality from what it perceives through very limited senses. It has fooled us all. Fortunately, we are awakening from a very narrow awareness to something deeper and more profound. That is the message of this book. In truth, *we* are the reality we seek. We are gods whose voices can only be heard in stillness and hush. Those who hear it, as I did, will surely know it. It will shake the foundation of their souls and they will lose their lives of construct, illusion, and personal history. What they find in its place will surely change the world. We all have this within us. It is our birthright to know God and, lo, when we come to a full realization of that truth, our inner divinity will awaken within us, for *there* it has always been.

I would like to offer a couple of final notes. First, I refer to God in the general sense and so any reference to "Him" or "Her" is not intended to imply the sex or any particular nature of God. I am not making any claim that God is a Him or a Her. It is only used as a reference as is the term 'God' throughout the book. How you personally view God is a matter I leave entirely up to you.

Additionally, I often cite the King James translation of the Old and New Testaments and I make reference to the words of Jesus many times throughout the book. I use these sources not as a Christian or as a follower of any other theological position but only as a reference to illustrate or point to Jesus "the man" as someone who clearly understood his own divine nature and only sought to make all of us aware that like him, so too, are we. I believe that Jesus, like very few before or after him, recognized the true nature of himself and of all mankind. In so knowing, he sought only to show us that he was not unique in any way and that we too are capable of doing anything he did or what we believe he can do. I have no religious or theological agenda of any kind. As I was raised Latter Day Saint (Mormon) I am, most familiar with Christian theology, Old and New Testament writings and with the man Jesus, whom I believe has been misunderstood and misinterpreted throughout those scriptures and in Christianity generally.

As in all spiritual writings preserved through the centuries, there are nuggets of profound and hidden truth—morsels to enlighten and uplift. If the reader can look beyond references as strictly "biblical" to the purity of truth, there will be no theological or dogmatic conflicts. As I mentioned earlier, this is an individual message that is applicable outside one's personal religious beliefs. Truth makes itself known to us in many forms and to the inner part of each of us that is divine, it matters not from whence it comes. I hope the words here help you in your quest to find God or whatever it is you search for.

Chapter I

Ye Are Gods

We, all of us, are gods. We all innately know this but have lost the knowing through conditioning to our current three-dimensional awareness. With a process that begins at birth and continues throughout our lives, we are conditioned by a never-ending circle of those who have gone before us and them by those before them. We go on to condition our posterity in the same awareness as our own. Our awareness deepens from generation to generation as new mysteries of the universe are discovered, enhancing a new understanding of what we experience in our three-dimensional awareness. Each generation surges forward, compounding the knowing of previous generations-"Line upon line, precept upon precept."

While the building of knowledge from generation to generation has improved life and made us more comfortable, it has not brought us closer to an understanding of that innate knowing that within each of us is our god who is dormant and buried under all the knowing we like to think has brought us closer and closer to God. It has not. In fact, it has led us ever further away from that innate knowing.

There have been many attempts to bridge the gap between science and religion or spirituality, but such efforts all focus on a knowing that lies outside the human soul. In other words, they look outward for three-dimensional answers that satisfy the physical senses. The nature of science is to put everything into three-dimensional context so that we understand nature, the universe, matter and God in terms we call rational. These rational terms translate to our physical senses of touch, smell, sight, sound, and taste. Outside of rational awareness, science fails to explain anything mysterious or that which falls outside that awareness.

Religion, on the other hand, has attempted to do much the same as science in its search for God but where historical tenants such as creation cross with scientific data such as evolution, religious leaders look to those historical tenants and ask that we have faith that somehow, some way, and at some point in time that science will be disproved and our faith will have saved us from the dark cloud of scientific or three-dimensional knowing. In other words, it is argued that "God will eventually prove us right." Neither can explain the miracles or mysterious acts of great spiritual figures, past and present other than to say they happen because they are something out there we have yet to be able to explain (scientific reasoning) or we don't know but "all things are possible to God" (religious reasoning).

Our conditioning makes it difficult to compete with the realities of science in three-dimensional terms and the mysteries of god in spiritual or religious terms. Both look outward for truth and answers to what god is thinking, overriding our own innate sense of self that knows we are so much greater than our science or religion allows us to be. Our sense of self knows "We" are the God we seek. *Each of us is God* with as much greatness and power as that with which we attribute to the unseen God out there somewhere in space and time or the heavens, as it were. At one time or another, we all know this about ourselves but the ever present conditioning effectively cancels out that knowing with the illusions we are trained to see and experience before us. Sadly, we search endlessly for something outside ourselves that really lies within. God eludes us in our present awareness even though he is always present. Knowing not the God we seek, she stands before us invisible to the three-dimensional senses we believe will discover her. She will not be discovered or known in the illusion we know as our current reality simply because this reality is *illusion*. This reality is superficial and does not account for that which this reality says *is not or cannot be real.*

It has been written metaphorically and literally in the Bible that we are gods, that we are greater than anything we have created God to be. Yet these teachings are explained away in such a way that supports the ongoing idea that we cannot be the gods that God speaks of because He is so much greater than anything man can conceive of. The words expressed in the Bible, however, could not be more explicit in their description of just how we became gods. In fact, the Bible begins with perhaps the richest story of "our becoming as the Gods" found in the very first three chapters of Genesis.

Looking at these words merits our attention. The story of the Garden of Eden and partaking of the fruit of the "Tree of Knowledge of Good and Evil" is metaphorically a description of *man* becoming *conscious* or coming to a heightened level of awareness he previously did not have. More concisely, man is now *knowing* that he *knows*. Think about *knowing that he knows?* What is *it* he now knows? What is *it* about which we *think? It* is everything that is within the view of our senses. Consequently, *everything,* or better yet, *anything* is the possible subject of our new *thinking.* Man becomes conscious and *everything* we can sense in our world becomes the subject of a new analysis that has never existed before, or at least that we were not aware of before. Think about the Garden of Eden. What was the condition of Adam and Eve while in the garden? Everything as we *know* it now existed in the Garden of Eden before we *knew* it. However, before we *knew* it, we didn't *need* to know it.

It was simply there. Everything was provided for the man and the woman and they could partake of the fruit of any tree save the "Tree of Knowledge of Good and Evil." Why the restriction of that tree? We don't find out until after they actually partake of the tree but in so doing they "became as one of us," *gods*, knowing good and evil. In other words, the man and the woman became gods. Yes, they awakened, became conscious, aware, suddenly *knowing* anew what they knew but did not comprehend in terms of this new *knowing*.

In simple terms, the God present in the Garden of Eden speaks clearly and declares that the man and the woman "have become as one of us." Put another way, "like us they have become gods" because they now have the same *knowing* as us—a knowledge of good and evil or infinite knowing.

If we consider the state man and woman were in while in the Garden of Eden, it is not unlike that of all wild creatures in their native condition. The mechanisms to survive are all in place. Everything they need (as in the Garden) is provided for them. There is no *thinking* in the sense of *understanding* why they do what they do. Creatures in the wild simply act. It is instinctual for them to do naturally what they do to sustain and fulfill their existence. All the mechanisms for a perfect fulfillment of life are in place. They are simply *provided for*, just like Adam and Eve in the Garden. Did thorns and thistles suddenly appear after they partook of the fruit? No, they were always there. Adam and Eve were simply not in a state of consciousness to where their *awareness* of such things mattered. If they could have *cared*, they *wouldn't* have cared. Creatures in their native environments don't need to care. They simply *do* what they are designed to do.

So what is it about *knowing* that made Adam and Eve, and consequently all of us who came after them, gods? This is a question that can only be understood by knowing the nature of God and if we consider that the God of Eden is the same as the God who created all things before creating the man and the woman and the Garden into which he put them, we can comprehend the meaning. "In the beginning, God created the heavens and the earth." The statement is straightforward, expressive, but profoundly meaningful. Simply put, *God creates.* Slice it again and it looks like all that is, all that we see, know, feel, and believe is a manifestation of what *God creates.* It might even be said that *all that is,* is the expression of a creative force that *saw* what was not and replaced it with what is.

Creating *what is* requires a knowledge of opposites. Opposites? Good and evil or contrasts. Good and evil is a metaphorical description of every *possibility* conceivable to mankind. It defines the spectrum of life possibilities available in our reality and encompasses the entire range of possible human experiences. It is the infinite knowing of gods! Good and evil are nothing more than a description of an infinite range of possibilities that conscious man was about to experience or *know!* The range of possibilities has always existed. We simply were not aware of it; indeed, we didn't need to be aware of it until *we* became "as the gods," or *we became gods.*

The "Tree of Knowledge of Good and Evil" could more appropriately be called the "Tree of Infinite Range of Possibilities." Good to evil and vice versa describes an unbounded series of possibilities and it is all neutral if viewed as a metaphorical *awakening* to that *range of possibilities.* As infinite beings in an endless universe where does one put *good* or *evil on such a spectrum?* We cannot. The spectrum of good and evil has no place on an immeasurable scale. Good and evil simply don't exist in infinite terms. They only exist in the three-dimensional terms we have applied to them.

From a few simple biblical phrases, we get a description of the entire range of experience—past, present, and future. Here it is: 1) God creates; 2) God *knows* opposites (good and evil or an infinite range of possibilities); 3) *Man is God.* Now the house of cards: If man is God and God creates, then man creates also. If the conceptual fuel of creation is knowing opposites (good and evil) or an infinite range of possibilities, then man's experience in *creating* is derived from that same conceptual fuel source or *knowing* as God also *knows*. In other words *"We are what we believe God to be."*

Let's clarify this idea in unmistakable terms that are indisputable. WE ARE GODS. *I am God. You are God.* You are not gods in embryo or sons and daughters of God or gods in the making or servants of God or subordinates to God in any way. You *are* God. You, I, all of us are made up of the exact *stuff* from which everything was created. That exact *creative* source of power, energy, intelligence, God or whatever you choose to call it is *us*. We are raw creative power and no power in the universe can ever take that away from us, not now, not ever.

If you are religious and conceptualize God in any form you choose: the image of man, spirit, devil, animal, unity of conscious— it matters not. You are god! If you are non religious and have a more worldly or scientific view of the nature of man-it matters not. You are god! What's more, you know it. You may not know it at the intellectual, analytical, cognitive, or spiritual level but this *knowing* is written into every particle of that which makes you what you are. What you perceive yourself to be may not be the god that you are but you are exactly the same as that which, at this very moment in time, causes the bursting forth of stars, galaxies and universes in spectacular explosions of creative power. Quite simply, your godliness *is*, and regardless of how you choose to think about it or not think about it, *you've got it.* Your *thinking* may deny it, but your biology does not. In fact, *you* are far greater than any God you can imagine or conceive of in your mind or dreams.

It is interesting that as God was making Adam and Eve aware of the new reality they would now be a part of, He seems to be addressing someone else who is apparently with Him. We never find out to whom He is speaking but it is made abundantly clear that this individual is also like God and that the man and the woman have also taken on the same attributes as they have. In other words "they have become as one of us." To *whomever* we give credit to for speaking the words of the gods of Eden, no scenario can alter the fact that *we, too, are gods.* If the words are believed as literal, then the "gods" have said "they have become as one of us." How can that phrase be interpreted any other way than that like them *we* are gods? If it is metaphorical and the words are meant to describe a process of *man* awakening to a new awareness, then that awareness is of a variety and abundance of unlimited possibility. In other words, *knowing* is "knowing as God knows." Our *knowing* is as great and extensive as God's knowing. Simply stated, *"Like Him, so are we."* We, therefore, are gods each of us in every way that He is.

We, for all of our modern progress and scientific advances, have not yet even begun to imagine the greatness we credit God with, and yet every bit of that greatness is available to us and infinitely more than that.

"Is it not written that ye are gods?" We are gods. "Ye are gods." We are not created in his image. If anything, we have created Him in our image and limited Him just as we have limited ourselves. We are so much greater than any image we can hold in our minds, even as infinite beings.

It is our beliefs that *we* are created in his (someone else's) image that limits us in *knowing* how great *we* are. Most of us cannot *think* beyond what we now see as *man* because we cannot get beyond the idea that since we are created in God's image that what we see is all there is. It was never intended to be like that. "They have become as one of us to know what we know and *be what we are.*" We are gods!

Chapter 2

The Sinless Nature of Gods

There is no sin, hence, we are all sinless. In this three-dimensional reality, there are only choices that have arisen out of the idea that knowing good and evil also includes judging between them. With the Christian belief that Man fell from grace and was now an errant creature ever destined to live a life of struggle, trial, and conflict, comes the concept of sin. Sin is believed to be the willful breaking of God's law even though when Adam and Eve were cast out of the Garden, they were not given a rule book outlining what constituted sin. They were only given to know an infinite range of possibilities that has been described as "good and evil." In other words, they were given "knowing," which is the ultimate gift of gods to be participants in the creative process and to enjoy the fruits of, not their labor, but of their thoughts, ideas and dreams. What a gift!!! We all possess this same ability to create our existence out of an unlimited spectrum of infinite possibilities.

However, we have limited ourselves because of our need not only to know the full range of possibilities before us, but also to judge what part of it is good and what part is evil. In the practice of judgment, we lose the ability to see beyond that judgment. In so doing, our thinking clouds our thoughts, ideas, and dreams in the reasoning of limited focus and unnecessary analysis. Judgment always produces a right or a wrong or a better or best result. Judgment is an individual scale derived from upbringing, schooling, life events, cultural and ethnic circumstances, which is, therefore, a finite scale that has wrapped itself around the vastness of infinity that surrounds us. In our need to determine the better of choices before us, we lose sight of boundless opportunities and a richness in life that is beyond anything we can imagine. Our need to *know* in three-dimensional terms what is good or what is evil is the creation of judgment in our lives and because of its finite nature we, unwittingly, limit ourselves to all that is possible.

As the story of Adam and Eve partaking of the fruit plays out, they are not accused of committing an act of evil nor are they told they have sinned after partaking of the fruit of the tree "of knowledge of good or evil." God did not exclaim their evil nature or condemn them in any way for sinning against him or anyone else. He did not introduce the idea that their act was good or evil in nature. They broke a command given to them by the creator of the garden who spelled out to them previously that to do so would bring about an awareness of their own death. In partaking of the tree from which they were commanded not to eat, not only were they not punished, they also became the same as that creator, knowing good and evil and becoming gods themselves. They were not judged in any way as we have been conditioned to believe. They were simply cast out of one creator's creation and given responsibility from that time forward to create their own existence as all gods do.

The idea that the man and the woman were judged in any way by the God of Eden is just not consistent with the biblical story. In fact, the story is perhaps most clear in presenting the idea that gods do not judge at all. Only "man" in his current state of assessing what is good and what is evil, judges in any way and places such characteristics on God. *Knowing* good and evil!! That was all the man and woman were given to know, not some divine insight in order to distinguish between them. Simply put, *there is no sin.*

According to Christian ideology, because of the original sin of Adam and Eve in the Garden and the innate sinfulness of mankind from that point forward, the God of Eden would now need to provide a way to save mankind from his sinful nature. The "way," as Christians believe, is that god would send His own son and cause him to suffer and die in the most cruel fashion as payment for not only the "sin" of Adam but for all the sins of mankind from that point on and into the future. If the Christian idea that Christ died on the cross for our sins is real and if such an act took place, then isn't that the same as saying there is *no sin*? If our sins are paid for by such an act, then how is that different from the idea that there is no sin? There is no sin. There never was sin and there never will be, regardless of the act committed or the judgments passed.

The idea of sin has its roots in the mistaken idea that human beings having become aware of "Good and Evil" would also *know the difference* between them. It was never intended to be that way. What came to pass with the idea of good and evil is that somehow man could be a wise and accurate judge of the difference. Man is not, nor was he ever intended to be, a judge of what constitutes good and what constitutes evil.

Consider also that Jesus even went so far as to teach us to forgive everyone. Why would such an act be necessary in a world where no sin exists? Jesus told us to forgive everyone because mankind has not "known" good and evil as He was instructed but also has attempted to judge it, put it on a scale, and condition all to accept it as divine or 'from god." Isn't the admonition to forgive everyone the same as saying there is no sin? Again, Jesus gives us another way to overcome our insatiable need to judge everything in existence on a scale of good or evil. Forgive everyone is the same as saying, "If you cannot accept the idea that there is no sin, forgive everyone of what you think or claim to be sin."

Jesus forgave everyone and told us to *forgive* everyone as He did. Why would He need to forgive anyone? Christians say He was perfect. He was perfect as are you and everyone else who has lived, lives now, and has yet to live. Jesus, who was quite possibly the most ideal incarnation that a human could ever attain in this life, was non-judgmental as He taught us all to be. What was He trying to convey to us by demonstrating the act of forgiveness?

It was His way to help us overcome our tendency to create rules and then to judge others according to them. To forgive is the answer given to those who judge. *Forgive* is the same as instructing, "*Don't judge.*" Judgment only exists where there are rules set that would prejudice us against another, be it another human, another culture, community, religion... whatever. Rules become the guidelines for *comparison*.

Comparison is the shadow of prejudice or bias. Prejudice or bias is the result of *breaking rules* which provides the need to *judge*, followed by castigation, followed by whatever *punishment* is meted out as a result of having *broken the rules*. *Breaking rules* usually means the addition of *new rules* for handling the breaking of the original rules. Rules beget judgment. "Judge not that ye be not judged." If you must judge, then forgive those you judge and if you can forgive, then you and whomever you have forgiven are without sin. It cannot be any clearer!! Jesus offered forgiveness as an *out* for judging, but the first great principle is not to judge at all – ever! Why? Because there is no *sin! Good and evil are not a scale to be used by those who want to judge the acts of others, but if you must judge good or evil then forgive those whom you have judged!*

Recall the story of the woman accused of adultery who was about to be stoned at the hands of her accusers. She begged Jesus to intervene on her behalf while her accusers prevailed upon Jesus to acknowledge their law as divine, but all He would do is acknowledge their law. "Yes, she has surely sinned against your law." So "let he who is without sin cast the first stone." No one dared be the first to cast a stone to which Jesus told the woman, "Go and sin no more." What was Jesus' motivation for such a comment? Because the reality of the current existence, as *created* by the leaders, laws, and rules of that time, was that the *breaking* of their *laws* constituted *sin* which, according to their law, required judgment followed by punishment. Christ was not telling the woman she was a *sinner*. He was telling her that in the "rendering of Caesar's what was Caesar's," or *law*, she best not break the *law* again as she would likely not to be spared as she was this time. The whole point of this story is the separation of, or *breaking away from* the idea that man-made laws constitute *sin* of any kind in the eyes of God (whose *real eyes, by the way,* are our own). God is only made to *care* at all about what we consider to be *sin* because *we* created that role for Him.

Jesus was intent on convincing the woman and each of us that we are not to live an existence of guilt and shame based on the bias created by man-made interpretations of what is right or what is wrong. *Man was given to know good and evil not be the judge of it!* The idea of sin in a realm of good and evil is ripe with the opportunity for all of us to attempt to judge the difference. But we are told not to judge at all.

Consider the Garden of Eden and the "Tree of Knowledge of Good and Evil." What is the point of this metaphor in the context of human existence? The story is a profound description of *how things came to be as they are,* but even more profound is its suggestion of *how things can be.* The symbolism is subtle but vivid as it describes the current condition of humans but equally vivid in its supposition that *as it now is, it need not be!*

What is the current condition of man? Everywhere you look, no matter where you look, the *knowledge* of good and evil is the essence of every *act* of man to find *meaning for* and *justification for* every *act* that has ever been made or every *act* yet to be made that our *knowing* will allow us to conceive of! Think about this? *Knowing* or *knowledge* is an *act* of *intelligence* or *intellect*. It is the machinations of analysis of *mind* upon various acts and conditions as perceived through a lens of *right* or *wrong* or *good and evil*. The symbolism of the tree spoken of in the Garden of Eden is not that *sin* was introduced as an act of *good or evil* for partaking of the fruit. It is a metaphor for the condition man now exists in. The *new* condition is simply that *man* now has the mind or cognitive ability to *process* acts and events in a new and analytical way or as *opposites*. Man can now override the old way of processing data which was to simply allow or accept whatever was happening as nothing more than an act that occurs without any judgment as to it being good or evil. In other words, "what is, simply, is."

There really was no *thinking* in the garden—rather just *being*. Partaking of the "Tree of Knowledge of Good and Evil" set into motion the process of *thinking*, of *comparing* things, acts, events, etc. relative to other things, acts, events, etc. The process of comparing leads to the process of *judging* which in its simplest form is nothing more than *deciding* the *better* of two choices: good or bad. It probably started with simple judgments about what plant was better to the taste or what made you sick versus what made you feel good, but it has developed into a formidable aspect of life as we now know it. In our need to judge the events and actions of others or life events, we have filled our minds with unnecessary ideas about good and evil that should have no place in our lives whatsoever. Judgment creates in our minds absolute criteria that negate any alternative except that which we have determined to be right or wrong. Absolutes confine us to a finite view of our existence and strap us to the limits of that view. How can we possibly suppose that our view in any context is the only right view? Is this not an absurdity?

Gods do not dwell in absolutes. Infinity has no place for absolutes. Any definition given to the goodness or badness of an act is to attempt to create absolute rules in a realm of infinity. There simply is no place on any "infinite scale" that you can place any act of individuals, nations, worlds, or universes. Good and evil as a scale is an abstract idea that has no place in the infinite realm of gods. Sin cannot exist when speaking in infinite terms and it is only in the finite *thinking* of man that such a concept can exist. However, as mentioned previously in the context of finite degrees, man tries to categorize events and acts. Yet we are asked first not to judge and secondly, if we fail at *not judging* we are asked to *forgive*. Either will cause a release of the energy required to hold the act in our consciousness and will free us of the responsibility of being "our brother's keeper." It will also free us from the guilt we all suffer because we have accepted the idea that sin exists and that we all sin.

Guilt is a terrible bedfellow and it can only exist in a world where there is an artificial demarcation between what we determine is good versus what is evil. Without the idea of sin or good and evil, there is no guilt and that is as it should be. Why else would Jesus ask us to forgive if it were not for the guilt we associate with it? We can break rules devised by man to maintain order and structure in human societies, but we cannot sin against those rules or any concept of good or evil constructed by the mind of man. Guilt, defined as remorse, self doubt, accepting responsibility for *sinful* acts or the violation of moral codes creates anxiety, stress and a false sense of our true nature as gods. It causes needless attachment to a reality that only sees the here and now through eyes that are conditioned to a very limited view of the world. Such a view has accepted, for whatever reason, the idea that as human beings, we are limited, sinful, and in need of some form of saving by someone or something outside our control.

It was so important to Jesus that we move beyond any idea of condemning ourselves in the context of society's rules ("render unto Caesar") or any idea about what was good and what was evil that He even went to the extreme of sacrificing Himself as the price to be paid for our own guilt at breaking nonexistent rules and laws that constitute *sin* in the finite minds of men. "If you cannot accept that you are without sin and set yourself free of the guilt you have over it, give your sins to me and then get over the guilt!" "I will take all your sins onto myself if you will let them go."

Therein, however, lies the problem. The idea of "having no sin" or "giving your sins over to someone who will take them" is not as easy as it sounds. *Most cannot give up the guilt!* It has become too much a part of their identities and thus nearly impossible to let go of. Guilt may be the single biggest factor in concealing our innate knowing of the god within. Guilt has a voice that is as strong as any voice we hear. Guilt is always there to remind us of our lowliness should the god within ever seek to get out. "You can't possibly be a god, look what you've done!!!" "You'll go to hell for even thinking such things."

Most Christians who have confessed, as it were, their sins and have accepted Jesus as the ransom for them cannot give up the guilt that comes with the conditioning that we are sinners and because of it we are *less than*. It might even be where the idea that "we are all sinners" comes from as it provides some sense of security (in numbers) that we are all the same and will all suffer a similar fate for our so-called sinful acts. Actually, the idea that we are all sinners is no different than stating that none of us are sinners. Since there is no good or evil, in infinite terms, what is the difference between being all good or all evil? There isn't. It all simply *is* and whatever we do, say, or think matters not. Life continues.

Guilt is like a leech sucking the life-force right out of us and the more rigid we are with our concepts of good, evil, and sinfulness, the greater our guilt and the more difficult it is to free ourselves from it. Jesus knew this. He knew the difficulty of pulling ourselves free of our own demons of guilt that literally drain our energy and cause us sorrow, pain, and stress over a lifetime. The negative emotions carry over from generation to generation setting the stage for each new generation to never know their godlike nature.

We must overcome the idea that there is sin anywhere in the world or in any act or event. In so doing, we must overcome our conceived notion that we will be judged by a God who dwells somewhere out there in the heavens and who watches us and cares in any way about our acts. We must peel away the layers of guilt and discover the magnificent and wondrous creatures we are. We are gods without beginning or end, blessed with divinity not unlike that which we ascribe to the various gods we have created in our own image. We must find that place within that houses the god that we are and keep guilt from ever seeping back into that part of our being. If there ever were a sin, it is that we have allowed *sin* to exist or that good and evil have any place in our vocabulary other than to describe the infinite range of possibilities before us all. As gods we don't confine our reality; *we bask in it!*

Chapter 3

Judging Good and Evil

Losing self to find life

The idea of sin, coupled with our demarcations of "good and evil," requires us to be judges both individually and collectively. Our modern day reality is wholly transfixed in the illusion that there are opposites in all things. With these opposites, we must identify the best between them in such a way that our conscious reckoning with everything in our lives must be categorized in some way so that all things have and are in their proper place. The concept of opposites creates a false competitiveness in our world that causes each of us to have a judgmental perspective of all things. It is part of the illusion we have been conditioned to see and almost a requirement to be accepted in any walk of life.

Judging the actions of others prevents us from ever seeing beyond the limits of our own reasons for making judgments in the first place. This is its inherent flaw. Judgment is a finite quality of the illusory life that we are conditioned to accept and be a part of when in reality, in infinite terms, there are no opposites. All is good! Nothing in all of creation, visible or invisible, has any need of any form of judgment because it is all good. In fact, it is wondrous and profound, and it is incredible just to be connected to it. In all of creation there is not one thing, not a single particle that is not without indescribable beauty! Our attachment to the *idea* that evil exists in the world *is* the evil. If we believe such things as the acts of human-on-human violence, natural disasters where many suffer or die, or any other part of our reality we accept as evil, it is due to the conditioning of life that has taught us it is so. It is difficult to comprehend that everything is as it should be when we have been taught to judge between good and evil. No one likes to see unnecessary suffering and yet in our collective reality, it is all around us. Great natural calamities occur and we surmise that evil has found place in our reality and we fight against it as if *battling* what we see as evil is the *good* that must overcome it. Again, good and evil is a description of an infinite universe where all things are not only possible but probable. Our need to judge between the two is where we lose sight of infinite life. We are born and will die in this reality and we fear death only because we have been taught that birth is a beginning and death is an ending. They are not! We are infinite and live forever and in living forever, we experience all things imagined and impossible to imagine. To judge any act of man or nature as evil is to attach ourselves to outcomes that on an infinite scale simply do not matter in any reality. Judging, in any form, confines us to a very narrow view of reality and places limits on us even though we are unlimited beings—even gods!!

When we have let our reason define the world we see, our mental nature will defend that reason rigorously, and sometimes even to the death. To judge requires us to look at the concept of good or evil and place our own and others' actions, thoughts and intentions, on a scale that confines those actions, thoughts, and intentions within the limits of that scale, thus preventing us from seeing anything beyond it. The idea of good and evil has been misunderstood as something definable in human terms when it is really a description of an endless spectrum of possibilities. Good and evil are really two sides of the same coin. They cannot be separated just as every single being living on this planet has within the self the same capability to do what we might label 'evil' as he does 'good.' In infinity, all things are possible and all is good. Where we go wrong is in seeing good and evil as opposites and supposing that we or anyone can possibly know where the line is drawn that separates the two.

There is no right or wrong; hence, there is no scale restricting us from seeing beyond what we see in our current state as judges. When we cast off the idea that things have opposites and that we have been divinely inspired to judge the better of those opposites, we open the window to the universe and we literally awaken to the idea that we are indeed infinite creatures without limits of any kind. When we overcome the idea that our *reasoning* must have *reasons* to judge, we overcome the limitations we create for ourselves by that reasoning. We must literally fight against our own sense of reason because of its ability to limit our perception to a very small area. It might be said that all things are possible to those who reject their own reasoning and the judgments they make based on that reasoning. Overcoming our need to judge and the idea that there are opposites in the world is the door through which infinity is found. Sin only exists in the world because we, in our finite reasoning, have decided there is a line between good and evil and have placed ourselves as the judges of that line. It is not so and never has been.

"Judge not that ye be not judged." This admonition has nothing to do with the idea that "as we judge others, so they will judge us," or that *God* will judge us likewise. When we judge, whether it be our own pointing finger or what we assume is God's judgment, we *feed* our reason, and make it stronger. In essence we judge ourselves, thus limiting ourselves to a very narrow *scale* that confines us to a *finite* existence when the *infinite* is our birthright. Gods have no limitations nor do we except those we place on ourselves. Gods place no limitations on themselves because they have no limitations! Gods understand their infinite nature and so must we. No scale of right or wrong can exist in an infinite reality! *Good and evil simply do not fit into infinity!!*

Judging is also an act of self importance. To place the value of our reason against the actions or thoughts of others is to place a value of a finite nature on an otherwise infinite spectrum of possible thought or actions available to every human. It is to set the scale we choose as the *correct measure over all others!* How absurd to think that we have an internal cognitive ability that makes our judgments better than anyone else's!

Nothing we do is of *infinite* importance. Little we do is of *finite* importance. Self importance is the bedfellow of our reason. To consider our scale of reason as an absolute, or the most sound above all others is the grandest act of self importance we can attain and consequently the most debilitating, self-limiting thing we do in this life. To condemn is to be condemned. To judge is to be judged. To limit is to be limited. Self importance is to allow ourselves to be controlled by a very limited sense of reason we create on our own and has a very narrow view of what is really going on around it. We create the limitation and then yield to it and by yielding to it, we further decrease our ability to see beyond our own importance. Self-importance feeds itself by attracting confirmation and support to bolster its finite conclusions concerning this reality. In other words, we become more locked into the idea that what we perceive is all there is. We accept the finite nature of this reality and confine ourselves to the idea that we cannot go beyond it.

Accepting the idea of opposites creates the finite world we have come to believe in. Fear grips us because not knowing what lies beyond this life is daunting and mysterious and yet the idea of infinity is just as daunting. Our finite reasoning resists the idea that we never really die and that everything continues on in some form. The idea that within each of us is the god we seek is so contrary to what we have been conditioned to believe that the mention of it is to blaspheme against the finite god we think we know and believe in. In a way, our finite reasoning protects us from the awesome power and responsibility of being God—of accepting our divine nature and seeing beyond the reality we have come to know. Opening ourselves beyond our limited reason would require us to cross into an unfamiliar realm where there are no limitations. Most of us have never experienced such vastness of possibility and find it difficult to comprehend. For some, the conditioning is so complete that it is in fact incomprehensible and to even consider it is unimaginable, and so they search for solace and comfort in the realm of the finite. Acceptance of the finite nature of this reality removes the responsibility of having to accept one's own journey through life. It protects us from having to look beyond any idea that the world of our five sense awareness is all there is. In such a state, we willingly give ourselves over to the collective minds that best suits our own finite beliefs. We yield our divine nature to the reasoning of others who think that what they know is somehow what we should believe. We become a number in a belief system we think provides comfort, security and answers to life's most mysterious questions. Funny thing about finite reason—it can only find security in numbers. It is never certain. The judgments we make over the choices we accept become the essence of all our sorrows, suffering and sadness in this reality. If we choose wrongly, according to our or others judgments, we suffer from the guilt prescribed for such acts. We often confess that in so choosing we are humbled before our fellow man. This is believed to release us from the guilt, but in reality, it is in acquiescence to the choices we believe are before us and that our judgment of those choices was in error. For most, the guilt never leaves but it contributes to other acts judged wrongly over a lifetime and becomes a part of our history of missteps. It further confirms our lowliness and lack of perfection and pulls us further away from accepting our true divine nature.

Judging our acts, and being remorseful for them, as good or bad or evil is not an act of humility. In fact, it is the opposite because it places unwarranted importance on ourselves as if our acts, good or bad, could ever have any real affect on anyone else. In our illusory reality, the acts of others do affect us but only because we let them and only because we fail to see our own divinity. That failure overlooks the wider range of possibilities, even *infinite possibilities* associated with such acts. We let others hurt us because we have tied ourselves to their acts through our reasoning which in turn sets out to make judgments about everything within the purview of that reasoning. Not only does it bind us to the acts of others and the supposed effects they have on us, but also it diverts us from the importance of *new* acts before us and a myriad of creative possibilities which is where we should always be focused anyway.

Judgment is the vehicle that gives order and structure where none *should* exist if we all could come to appreciate our godlike potential. Judgment may be necessary to maintain an orderly society, but it should never be accepted as a delineation between good or evil. There is no, nor will there ever be, a judgment about what is sin because *there is no sin!* We must overcome the idea of sin and rid ourselves of the need to judge by coming to a simple *knowing* that things, all things, are as they are and that is *all* they are supposed or need to be.

Judging is a wholly human activity and consequently overlooks any spiritual needs or outcomes. It is grounded in the five physical senses and while that might be the only fair or accurate way for the physical reality we live in, it has a tendency to support the idea that if we can't see it, smell it, taste it, touch it, or hear it that it cannot be. Judgment takes on the same forms of proof as science in that it only functions within the realm of the physical senses as the framework into which all things must fall in order to be understood. Many of our religious institutions promote that idea and interpret such concepts as *gifts of the spirit* to be not of God but of the devil only because they do not fit a narrow definition of what they have defined as good. Thus *judgment* limits them from ever accessing such gifts because it sees them as evil or unbefitting the guidelines of the institution. One of our best examples of this comes in the form of our own religious beliefs. People have become so far removed from the idea that they are divine that they have accepted that an institution, they happen to follow, is the only outlet for anything great or miraculous to occur. Jesus, Buddha and many other spiritual teachers, throughout history, taught a wide ranging message of *individual* greatness not predicated on anything other than believing it to be so. We have heard their various messages that we are all capable of the, seemingly, impossible but have fallen into a belief that, unlike us, they were extraordinary and unique. They, themselves, taught that all of us were unique and capable of anything they were able to do and even more. Somehow in all the translations of sacred writings and the creation of religious and secular institutions we have lost what they knew about themselves and each of us as well, that is that we are gods.

Another example is that there are many among us who feel the presence of other realities and while they are unable to describe them with language, as we know it, or perhaps to not even comprehend them in any way, they simply know of these realities and that *realness* is as meaningful to them as anything they *know* through their physical senses. They simply know, but the prevailing tendency is to describe in some way, something that is coherent and meaningful to the physical senses. It often cannot be done and what's more is that *judging* is the only reason we think it needs to be done!

The very act of judging in any form obscures everything our physical senses are really capable of knowing or perceiving, let alone non-physical sensing. How can we ever hope to know something if we can't accept someone's *knowing* that we have judged *unknowingly*?

Gods are non-judgmental and in being so, any god outside *the god that we are* cannot have a role in our lives. In other words, if your belief is that there is a God who exists in the traditional sense somewhere out there, that God cannot have a judgmental role in your life because gods have no need of judgment of any kind. Non-judgmental gods have no need to be keeping score or a record of your life. Your life is what it is and it is completely of your own making. You are completely responsible for everything that happens in your life. Neither God nor anyone else you believe in has influence over you. No judgment of any act you have committed or will commit will ever stand up in a universal court where God is the judge simply because God will not judge.

If gods do not judge, then why do we? This really is the crux of the matter. In our reality we have been conditioned to see every act as good or bad or maybe better and best. This conditioning carries over into every aspect of our lives, and those things that we adhere to as good or bad become the anchor upon which we judge our own actions. In other words, we condemn ourselves because of the things we have come to accept are evil or bad. Coupled with our own judgment is the pain and guilt we attach to the violations we judge ourselves guilty of. Like guilt, judging drains energy more than anything else; this is why Jesus spoke so adamantly against it.

"Judge not that ye be not judged" is not about tit for tat – "if you do it to me, I can or someone else will do it to you". It is, rather, that in judging others, you drain yourself of the energy expended to judge. As long as you hold the judgment, the energy lost will never come back. Think about it. We do not need to judge. We don't have to form judgmental opinions about anything, but only we can choose not to do so. Not doing so attaches us to the actions of others and gets us personally involved in their lives instead of focusing on all the possibilities available to us individually. We are not asked to be our brother's keeper in the act of creation. Create only your own experience and revel in it while leaving others alone to create their own experience. The energy utilized to focus on others leaves you and feeds them and vise versa. Judging is one of the most pervasive but subtle ways we turn our energy, our focus onto others and create a level of self importance in ourselves. "I am the better judge because I am right and you are wrong."

Jesus' life exemplifies a life that didn't care about the things we have come to believe are important. "Consider the lilies of the field; they neither toil nor spin and yet Solomon in all is glory was not arrayed as one of these," said Jesus. He also told us to "Take no thought for tomorrow." In other words, all the things we consider important to our reality such as our homes, cars, education, affiliations, social status, job, appearance, etc. are of no consequence when viewing the bigger *life* picture. The bigger picture transcends anything we consider important in this life and we have access to it when we let go of those things that bind us to this reality. It is not to say that we cannot have abundance in this reality. It is only that the things we do have should never override our greater sense of awareness that we are gods and are arrayed with so much more than we could possibly acquire or attain in this life. It is the drive to obtain, hold onto, and increase that diverts our energy from the infinite to the finite. Jesus showed us that we do not need such things in our lives and that doing so drains us of the power He was able to use to perform the miracles He did. Judging drains our power because it makes the things in this reality all important to the exclusion of anything else. The act of judging requires that we put energy into things that are external to us and in reality inconsequential. When His disciples came to Him inquiring about "others" who were casting out demons but not in His (Jesus') name, they had not understood that Jesus was not the only vehicle through whom such things could be done. They were still caught up in the duality that "our" way is the right or only way. Jesus' response was of unconcern. "Leave them alone for they are not against us." Jesus had already explained that everyone had power comparable to and even greater than any power He had. Many who subscribe to Christian beliefs today are still of the idea that the only way is through Jesus as opposed to what He really taught—and that was that we are gods and that anything we ascribe to God we have within ourselves. In order to realize our god-like natures, we must overcome our need to judge others. Judging draws us in to a never ending duality that will remain unresolved. It is an endless loop that will take every ounce of energy you are willing to give to it and never return it nor satisfy any supposed need you may have in the resolution you think exists!!

As gods we need not worry about our brothers and sisters with regard to all the things they involve themselves in that we think must have a label of right or wrong. We need not consider any act of individuals or collectives of individuals as being good or evil. Life is infinite and beyond any judgment we could possibly consider. Infinite possibilities mean infinite outcomes. All of that is before us and is ours if we let go of the part of our reality that says we have to "care enough" to judge others according to our reasoning. We are not to judge, not because of any impact it has on others but because of the impact it has on us. Gods can only exist in a neutrality that makes no judgments about anything going on and accepts unconditionally every act or event as just a part of the infinite range of possibilities before all of us and all of creation. We must develop the capacity to do the same for therein lies our own acceptance of all that is and our ability to take responsibility fully for everything that happens or that we do in this life. When we eliminate judgment from our lives, we open the doors to infinity and in so doing, we find the divine within us. The divine is everywhere before us but it is us, also! Look through infinity and find God—find yourself.

Chapter 4

When Gods Become Human

The serpent beguiled me and I did eat

Reflect on the story of the creation, specifically on the first man and woman and the events occurring in the Garden of Eden as recorded in the first few chapters of the Book of Genesis. It is also in these few chapters that we learn of the serpent's deception of Adam and Eve. Consider the arguments used by the serpent to convince Eve to partake of the fruit of the tree. The chatter about *not dying* and becoming as gods knowing good and evil, and the remark that the fruit is good for food and pleasant to the eyes is all part of the serpent's persuasive strategy. The serpent draws Eve into a discussion of the three-dimensional elements of the tree that she was either unfamiliar with or knew previously about but had not considered in terms the serpent now brought to her mind. The serpent encourages a thinking process governed by duality that seeks to find the *better* of all the choices we see before us. Such an existence of duality would cause man to make choices, creating a competitive environment and an endless dialog that would plague man from that point on. The new character in the life of man was no longer the voice of God he heard on a regular basis, but another voice that would challenge everything the voice of God would say. That new voice is the voice of ego.

There was no serpent! What is the subtle beast spoken of then? It is the thinking, chattering mind of man. The serpent is the constant voice of the cognitive mind. It is the ego, the processor of all our sensory inputs, and, ultimately, the protector of itself. Consider the sensory nature of the discussion between Eve and the serpent. God, on one hand, warns "Do not eat of the tree as there will be consequences if you do." The serpent, on the other, entices Eve: "Look at how beautiful the fruit is and think of all the things eating it can bring to you, not the least of which is that it tastes good. It will open your eyes to new seeing, the very seeing that God sees. You will be like Him." There was no serpent beguiling Eve. Her own thinking did, and after partaking of the fruit, she went to Adam and gave to him using all the reasons her own thinking presented to her previously. It is at this moment that the real serpent (of the mind) becomes active, filling their heads with the idea that they are naked and will need new clothes and hiding places and subsequently introduces blame and finger pointing. This new awareness they comprehend includes all the egocentric structures we see active today in all our dealings as humans such as guilt, shame, fear, anger, and doubt. These are endless emotional states we identify with because we are conditioned to engage in them by egos other than our own from the moment we are born. Just like newborn children, Adam and Eve were innocent and pure in every way until they were inundated by the egocentric structures of the world that constantly pit one thing against another.

Isn't it interesting that God does not destroy the serpent or cast it out forever so it can never again affect the man or woman? No, He dispatches it with a curse (the only real curse in the story) and promise that the seed of the woman would have power to crush its head while leaving it around to bruise their heels. It has no real power over the seed of the woman, but remember that the serpent is subtle, more subtle than all the beasts of the field. So subtle is the ego that it talks even when we aren't consciously listening and its purpose is to preserve itself in anyway it can. It uses all the same reasoning techniques it used originally on Eve.

Rationalizations, lies, reasoning coupled with logic and learning, finger pointing, blame, deception and score keeping—these are the ego's tricks. Its original game of defining right and wrong is its most subtle stratagem to convince the mind of rightness or wrongness, even good and evil. It even supposes that it alone can determine true right or wrong and accurately define the line between good and evil, even though no such line exists. The ability of the ego to persuade its host that a duality of good and bad exists everywhere is its most formidable device for staying hidden from our power to crush its head.

Ego cannot exist in a world of neutrality where everything is considered equal. It must be able to pit two things against one another preferably something weaker than itself but it is just as content with something stronger. Opposition is what the ego needs and seeks. The duality of good and evil are the playground of the ego and it thrives in this seemingly naturally competitive arena where it easily nourishes and fuels itself. Its deception is so subtle and complete that most of us, both individually and collectively, have been lulled to sleep and live in a reality that is illusory, mysterious, and competitive. We are asleep so soundly that we rarely, if ever, wake up.

Ego will even go so far as to create the circumstances in which it can point a finger of *righteous indignation* at anyone who disagrees with its viewpoint and in a show of moral certitude and holiness, assumes the role of "the defender of the faith," as it were, and upholder of what is good and holy. This all goes on and we don't even know it. It has become so second nature that we even look to ego as our ultimate identity. If someone points out to us that we are all deceived by ego, it (ego) immediately springs into defensive mode to point out again and again our true grip on reality and that any such deception could not possibly be part of our make up. "How dare you accuse me," ego exclaims!

We all slither and crawl on our bellies as the serpent of Eden was cursed to do. We all yield to the egotistical voice and pretend to hide from it when exposure is imminent. Just as Adam and Eve hid, so too do we hide as much as our ego self can in order to spare it any embarrassment or shame of exposure. It is impossible to know anyone's true history and so the ego survives virtually unbeknownst to anyone outside the perfect world it wants everyone to think exists as we perceive things through our physical senses. What it doesn't want us to remember is that other world in which God freely walked with the man and the woman in the "cool of the day," the world of true being or self and the world of truly knowing who we are.

Ego is the necessary evil of our current existence. That is because everybody has one and it requires an ego to function in a world of other egos. The game of deception cannot be played without them and it is a game of deception. The game of ego is to mask reality by presenting masks to the world for all to see. We all wear differing masks depending on the requirements of any given situation. For instance, when we go to work we may act in such a way that is completely unlike anything we might do when visiting with friends or with our children or grandchildren. We may wear a mask of piety when we attend church or synagogue that comes off when we attend our favorite live sporting event or other activity. We grow up learning what mask to wear, what it means, and how we should act when others are wearing theirs. On every level, ego creates mystery and attempts to hide our innate *oneness* with all that is or has ever been. Ego knows its place but is so adept at convincing us that it is our true identity that it keeps at bay the intuitive nudges from within that we are gods with power beyond anything the ego can construct through its endless chatter. Even in the garden where God spoke to the serpent and cursed it, there was a knowing that it had escaped total annihilation. Yet even in its weakened state, it continues to "bruise the heel of man" by subtly overcoming the intuitive voice of God with its own voice of three-dimensional knowing. On its belly it would go and as the serpent goes, so have we.

What is so astonishing is how overt the noise of ego is and still we almost never hear it. In truth, it never stops and is so incessant that it has overrun us with the things that are important and meaningful in life, at least from its ground-slithering vantage point. Ego has created the idea that our ability to think is what separates us from all other creatures in existence. Thinking, or more specifically, our ability to attain a high and complex level of cognitive thought, is what separates us from other animals or so this is how we see it. This is what we have come to accept in our so-called enlightenment—"I think therefore I am." We have institutionalized thinking and the constructs of our egos to the point that it has become impossible to put ego back where it belongs, on its belly, eating dust. This is not to say there is not a place for thinking in the course of our lives. Thinking should be considered a tool that is accessible when needed to resolve computational problems such as math equations, engineering design details, and other problems of that nature. Thinking is not a tool to sort out life's deeper questions or to find ones own true inner self. Our greatest honors are bestowed upon those we consider great thinkers, larger than life egos, and yet in all their thinking could any of them walk on water as did Jesus? The egocentric mind, the thinking, chattering mind is not the key to the kingdom, no matter how much we institutionalize, honor, and protect it.

Virtually every institution of life has become an institution of thinking, and yet people everywhere continue to be as distant and separated from *God* as ever. Ego has even been brash in its promise to man that any state that he aspires to, be it physical, mental, or spiritual, can be achieved, and for only a small price. Bodies can be younger and stronger; minds can be quicker and more sound; and our spiritual needs can be cared for at any spa or retreat—complete renewal, anytime, anywhere. Egos have developed egos that can assure other egos that they can be honored and respected as they unmask just long enough to undergo renewal that promises vitality, happiness, and rebirth. In other words, institutional egos have been created to convince individual egos that all egos are sensitive and fragile and should be handled at all times with great care and feeling. They have given us proper and specific ways to approach and handle the sensitivity of the ego so as to not damage in any way something so fragile. They have created a way to help others unmask so that others who are masked can offer nourishment and revival without damage or stress. As mentioned previously, we wear masks that are created for the various situations in our lives and they only come off so we can put on another appropriate to the circumstances we find ourselves in. We have so many masks and we have become careful not to harm or *bruise* the ego in any way, contrary to the suggestion in Eden that we should crush its head. Much of our so-called political correctness is focused on this ever increasing sensitivity to the *bruising* of ego.

The serpent is subtle as is ego. Low and out of sight, it slithers along unnoticed by the many and finds its way into every aspect of life. The more things it gets into, the more trapped we become and consequently the more distant from our higher self that would be God. Ego traps us in endless chatter and constant doubt. This is its way (you will not die but shall surely live!). If enough doubt can be cast, the more reasons to look for ways or solutions to overcome it. The more solutions needed, the more chatter. It is not a covert scenario the ego operates in. In fact, it is chronically overt, but it goes unnoticed. We only have to stop what we are doing for a few minutes and quiet ourselves and listen. Just listen to noise in the mind. It never stops. In fact, it is so insidious and explicit, very few people can ever successfully meditate because the mind, which has been on auto-pilot, will not stop its chatter. The ego knows there is something greater than itself. It was metaphorically spoken of in the garden. *The ego (serpent) knows God.* It knows we are gods and that we are creators of far more than we can possibly imagine, but it also knows that it cannot exist in that world. It cannot survive where its importance is second to a process it can have no part in. We have creative power that it cannot tolerate so it overwhelms the god within with so much noise, ultimately snuffing out any inkling we once had that it is our true nature to be as the god of Eden and cast it out of our garden, or our lives, forever.

Ego creates the duality of good and evil to undo its creative, godlike counterpart. Not to do so would be the final blow or crushing of its head. The ego has become very good at its own survival. Why would it go to the trouble to deceive the man and woman if not to ensure its own continued existence? "Talk with the woman. Get her thinking about all the possibilities available with this simple act of eating the fruit." This strategy is cunning and its success is evident when we consider any institution on earth. Such institutions are all virtually bastions of the ego of man. In fact, they are the mechanisms created by thinking man to fuel his ego. Rare is the individual who has crushed the head of his ego, so rare, indeed, that we don't even recognize them until they are gone: Jesus, Buddha, Mohammed, Lao Tzu, Padre Pio, Dalai Lama, to name a few.

They all understood that egocentric man had no way of ever realizing his true godlike potential in the noise and chatter of thinking and that such an endeavor was futile without shutting it down and tuning into real self. The true self has power over ego, but it must be heard over the noise of ego or it cannot call upon the creative power or energy of the universe, a power that is inherently ours as part of our creative and godlike nature.

Isn't it interesting that partaking of the fruit of the tree would set a course of events into motion that would launch man out of the garden and into creative life without any limitation, and yet at the same time of that incredible awareness, the ego too would be launched and over time, inexorably, would darken the awareness and tie us up in endless chatter so as to dull us to our true nature, and prevent us from ever connecting to the creative power we all possess within?

Sadly, we have accepted the description of the life we choose without ever becoming aware because in its subtleness, the ego is driven to prove through invention and discovery that it knows the way and can lead us to a place of full awareness through its constructions. It cannot, but the ego never ceases trying. It has to, or it will lose its edge. The structures of modern man bear out the ego's ability to push itself beyond incredible limits and all of our modern conveniences, devices, and means of communication pale in comparison to what our creative godlike abilities could produce. Egotistical drive, scientific achievement, and all the breakthroughs of modern man have been impressive. Carl Sagan underscores this efficiently: "Science has produced the goods." Our world, a creation of the ego drive to stimulate and protect itself, is truly remarkable and few can argue with the vastness of enterprise and commerce modern man has attained. Life has become simplified, convenient, and productive. The ego has quietly absorbed all of these achievements of modern man and pushed itself ever farther from its nemesis, the god within.

Knowledge of our physical world and of the universe increases year by year. Our ability to reach out into the universe, to study its beginning, and to theorize about its ending is unlike anything ever conceived of in human history. We can grow smarter and more aware every day, but of what? Science has truly delivered "the goods" and answers what religions have tried but were unable to in terms of all the modern conveniences we know. However, as much as the enlightenment of science and religion have provided to the modern world with, why does there continue to be so much despair, unhappiness, and a yearning for something greater? Why does there always seem to be some other kind of convenience or abundance that is missing from our lives? Why do we so aggressively forge ahead, searching endlessly for *that something*, as we do, if all is so well?

It is because experts in the fields of science and religion, while saying that they want to know the mind of God or to find a "theory of everything," are really ego driven and as such, drive to create a world that satisfies only the ego. Religious leaders protect the ego from ever dealing with itself by providing remedies for our shortcomings and restitution for situations they identify as good or bad, while scientists provide more *things* to comfort and coddle it.

Governments are formed to moderate the output of both and to protect us when they fail *and they always fail!* They fail because the nature of ego is not to preserve the physical man, although it must do this to survive, but to safeguard itself. The ego has to be constantly nurtured and protected, so it finds itself by driving man to a "better" this or that, but "this" or "that" is always something *out there.* Feeding the ego fails to let out the true self that is always *within* and never has the voracious appetite of the ego. The ego noisily *needs and feeds* while the true self quietly *knows.* Let me say that again: true self, the god within, q*uietly knows.* That might be a definition of humility—quietly knowing.

"Solomon − man, in all his glory, was not arrayed as one of these." True self has no need of anything *without* or outside the inner knowing of itself. All that is required is *quiet* to know that self and the knowing of that self is all that is essential to know God. God is within always and *only within.* There is no need for anything *without* to discover and know the power within or to know God.

There is no need for science, religion, government, or any other institution the ego of thinking man has created. We have the *stuff* of gods within us and it is ours for whatever we want. In fact, not only are we the stuff of gods, *we are gods!* Nothing is impossible or forbidden, nor should it be the concern of any individual or institutionalized ego.

The great metaphorical sin of man was not partaking of the fruit of the tree, nor was it listening to the serpent. It was giving in to the incessant chatter of the mind and giving rise to the insatiable ego of man. Why would God protect Adam and Eve from partaking of the tree of life by putting an angel to guard it? It can only be that God knew that the insatiable ego, the serpent of Eden would destroy itself in its aggressive need to nourish and preserve itself. God would truly be a cruel god if He let us continue in our current path without a means to get out of it. We have a way and it is through the discovery of our inner self. The answers we seek from science or religion can only be made known and understood by the god within. Inner awareness is the only way to satisfy our hunger for greater knowing! Satisfaction comes not from the inventions of science or the sanctions of religion, but rather from knowing your own divine nature.

The ego of man has delivered the devices to utterly destroy itself. We live in a time that reflects the ultimate insanity that ego can achieve, the ability to wipe itself out. The only reason it doesn't is because it knows that without a human host, it cannot survive. This collective egocentric insanity is the ultimate power and the only true power it has ever been truly capable of, namely its own destruction. Ego is always capable of destroying another to save itself. Individually or collectively, it must stand against something in order to live, even if the result is the annihilation of other individuals or collective egos. The egocentric mind must feed on other egos. Its ultimate path has lead to our current situation in the world. Our world is literally a "button push" away from annihilation of everything as we now know it. It is the only course the ego could ever take because it cannot let itself see where true power comes from, so it looks ever outward. If it were not for the ultimate fear the ego has created, that of death, the "button" would have been pushed almost immediately after the device to destroy the earth had been created. Fear of death is the only thing that has power to hold ego back from total annihilation and only because it would lose its identity that it has so carefully created in the world.

Outwardly, the ego looks for a way to overcome or end this madness, but it cannot. *It created the madness out of its own madness.* "Ego *is* the madness!" Operating from a vantage point of madness cannot lead out us of madness. It's the blind leading the blind. It can only get you more blindness, or madness.

The collective ego is as insatiable as its individual counterpart. It is also divisive and competitive, pitting itself against nations, governments, ethnicity, and institutions of every kind. The "chatter" of the collective is the noise of its individual constituents. Individuals scream out in defiance of their disagreeing counterparts and the noisy rhetoric becomes the fodder of politics, religion, governments, and every other institution of egocentric man.

Everything, indeed everyone, is wrong or right from one point of view or another and in the midst of these points of view everywhere in the world, we hear the shouting and screaming of ego. It is a paradox of magnificent scale that we accept without ever knowing it is of our own *individual making!* Everywhere you look nations and people are deceived by the subtleness and cunning of an egotistical drive that is relentless in its need to suspend any thought that we are above it all and hold the power to create a world in which we could all exist as the gods we are without judgments and noise of any kind.

I have always found it interesting that in developing the ultimate egotistical device capable of destroying our entire planet, the atomic bomb, that those who created it became the biggest advocates for never using it. It is almost as if the egos of these individuals, working collectively on behalf of another egoic collective, reached a breaking point or point at which the greater part of themselves, the god within, cried out in anguish that this could no longer go on. "What have we done?" The creation of the ultimate destructive force became the catalyst for looking inward for something greater to intervene and stop the madness. How interesting that in the mania of creating a device so massively destructive, they heard the voice of God pleading that they never use it! How do we hear such a voice?

The answer is in stillness, both individually and collectively. "Be still and know that I am God." In our own stillness, we can know that God is within. Within each of us right now that inner knowing is what can save us. Many the world over believe that Jesus came to save us and he did!! Not because we should believe in him or that our faith in him saves us. We are saved when we come to understand his teaching that "the kingdom of God is within us." It is not a person or place that will protect or save us from what ego is leading us to. Looking to Jesus, or to anyone for that matter, as a savior is an egocentric device. Remember, ego always looks outward. "Partake of the fruit of that tree and your eyes will be opened." "Over here, over there, this person or that one." Ego looks outward to the devices, stratagems, and locations of other egos, and yet the gift we all have is that within ourselves we not only have *knowing* but we also are gods having power to effect worldly change that the ego will never possess. We are our own saviors!

"The ground upon which we stand is holy ground." We are holy, each one of us. The kingdom of God is within each of us. We are gods eternal. Jesus was not instructing, "Believe in me." He was saying, "Believe *like* me! You have the same power I do and with that power you can do so much more than I have done. "I am come not to destroy the law but to fulfill it." In other words, his intention is that "I am come to show each of *you* that within you lies exactly the same as that which you see in me." Jesus never told his disciples that he was greater than them, nor extolled the miracles he performed. When healing the sick, he would say "Thy faith hath made thee whole." In other words, "*You have healed yourself.* Your *power* did this, not mine. He that believes, not in me, but *like* me will have eternal life."

Believe *like me* that you and your Father are one just as I and my Father are one. Who is the Father? The Father is the father of spirits. In other words, Jesus' father was his inner self or as he referred to it *spirit*. We all have a spirit, a life force, or energy that dwells within us. Some may think of it as the observer behind everything going on that quietly watches without interfering. That observer or one having awareness of all thought and action is the Father. That is God. That is who we really are when we are still and without any egotistical argument or fantasy. When the thinking is silenced and all that is left is quiet and stillness, the Father shows Himself. Our God shines forth and Lo! God was there all the time, always with us, waiting for us to simply quiet ourselves down so he could emerge.

The significance of Jesus' life is that *he got it.* "I and my Father are one." *I and my Father* equals God. I am God and so are you. That is his message! There is no place that you must go to or act you must perform that can lead you to God. He dwells within you, always has, and regardless of whether or not you ever find him, always will! Jesus got it in a way few other humans have. He crushed the serpent's head, quieted the noise of ego, and demonstrated the kind of power gods possess. He knew the complete oneness of Himself and the Father and the grand power of creation that extends *outward from the inward.* Again, he used power, not to demonstrate His greatness (that would have been an act of ego), but to demonstrate for us *our greatness!*

In fact, the whole story of Jesus is another example of how the egotistical mind has disenfranchised man. Jesus showed us in spectacular ways what creative gods are capable of. Every aspect of his public life (three years) was to this end, yet what has happened in the Christian world is exactly opposite. In the egocentric translation of the Gospels, not only can we not be like him, we cannot be *saved* without him! Again, we are looking *outward* to something that can only come from inward. Ego always looks outside the human form for reconciliation of its own inability to connect to the divine nature we all possess. Looking outward masks what is *inward* and is always there. This is the reason for our many masks. Masks project something unreal and fake to those outside us while hiding inner truth, but our conditioning has made this a necessary part of our reality.

Instead of acknowledging the divinity Jesus said we all had, equal to or greater than his own, ego has created Jesus in its own image as the greatest of all egos. This image is so great, in fact, that we cannot even begin to get close to what he was. We are sinners before him hopelessly lost forever unless we acknowledge him as the only one through whom we can find redemption for our sinful nature and under whose grace, only, we can be awarded a continued life. In other words, we are told we can never be like him but only with him. Another trick of the ego is to hold us down and keep us from exploring our own creative and godlike nature. Such is the nature of ego. "If I must go upon my belly, then so must you." I (ego) cannot look up and see the heights you are truly capable of being, so I will do everything possible to get you to look down. Here am I, down here." Ego is subtle, slithering, and well below the perceptive view of what we really are.

We are gods and the ego (serpent) knows it. It knows which gives it an edge in waging the battle that keeps us from knowing. It knows it must forever be about the business of outwardly pursuing anything it can to keep us convinced that we are neither powerful nor special, but instead are unworthy and in need of outward help, status, and recognition. It continues to create devices and stratagems to keep us in this place. It has convinced us that all the things we look to for credibility in this life, such as education, career or profession, income, social status, race or color, religion, are elevated in importance so we all have something to compare ourselves against in our so-called status in the human pecking order. The ego is so clever that it has even permeated the minds of religious leaders and the relevant institutions in such a way that as Jesus remarked, "Even the very elect are deceived." All are blinded *by* what appears to matter and oblivious *to* what really does matter.

Ask any religious leader, or look at the tenets of any religious institution, and they will provide an answer consistent with their understanding of dogma. It may even seem as if they know otherwise but simply will not veer from their conditioned ideology. Joseph Campbell tells the story of a meeting he had with an Indian gentleman who asked him what westerners were saying about the dating of the Vedas, or Hindu scriptures. In answering, Joseph Campbell told him that the dating was being assigned to the period of time 1500 to 1000 B.C. and he also pointed out that there was new evidence that there was a civilization older than the Vedas, to which the Indian gentleman replied, "I know, but as an orthodox Hindu I cannot believe that there is anything in the universe earlier than the Vedas." We see this type of religious devotion in all faiths regardless of certain knowing to the contrary. This is what it means to be oblivious to the things that matter! It is difficult to understand this type of zeal and yet we see individuals seemingly accept scientific truths and still hold fast to their religious conditioning.

Why do so many accept the answers of their religious leaders or their upbringing, knowing they are wrong? On the other hand, if their answers were right, why do so many continue to search as if they don't know or believe? Why does their reason fail to sooth or comfort us when we seek them for answers? In truth, we know why institutional *reason* fails. All of our egotistical constructs, rational as we think they are, remain grounded in scholarly study, contemplation, research, and accreditation; consequently, we always end up falling back to a discussion of *beliefs* or *the ever egocentric need to be right.* "I was taught this way, so that is how it is!" Often such discussions become heated and forceful to the point of being venomous, like a serpent spewing poison in every direction. Reason fails us because it comes from egotistical constructs outside ourselves that carry institutional acceptance and regard. Such acceptance and regard are requirements of the ego's need to feel good about itself and to be accepted among other egos. It fails because institutional acceptance has judged that *it*, the institutionalized ego, is solely qualified above any individual inner knowing and it always seeks to prove it in three-dimensional terms. Ego will ask that so-called inner knowing be proven for all to see. It asks for signs and miracles as proof but even when such are given, it still cannot accept them. Ego always finds a way to discredit them. It has to or it cannot exist.

Egocentric reasoning is almost always used to *explain things without* and is wholly inadequate for explaining unexplainable things *within*. Recall the story of the Scribes and Pharisees who asked Jesus by what authority do you speak and perform such things. His answer confounded them because they were looking for an institutional authority. In other words, they were asking him what school he went to or who was his teacher or master. Remember that his response to them was in the form of a question, asking by what authority had John the Baptist acted as he did. They had to think about their answer because John the Baptist was highly regarded by the people of that time. If they had answered that he was not a prophet, the people would have become upset. To recognize John as a prophet, however, would require them to accept that his authority really did come from God, which was something they could not do in the light of institutional authority that to them was all that mattered.

They chose not to answer because their own institutional qualifiers, their collective acceptance constructed by their egos, would have come under scrutiny and question. In other words, the institution or collective ego that creates the institution establishes the means by which someone can be called to any position of authority. All institutions are like this. They derive authority from the collective egos of individuals and become the voice of authority for those individual egos. We see this in every activity man undertakes including his governments. Jesus understood the limitations of institutional constructs and the limitations they place on human development. He also knew that they were aware that he had some special power that they and their institutions could not possibly describe or account for. This rattled them completely because by their reckoning, a completely egocentric reckoning, they had no way of explaining or even comprehending what Jesus was all about. For them, it simply was not possible that Jesus did what he did without sanctions from a recognized institution or individual.

How far does the ego go to protect itself and ensure the viability of the institutions it creates? Perhaps another story from the New Testament can illustrate how uncontrolled and desperate the ego becomes. Recall the story of Lazarus, the friend of Jesus, who after contracting some illness, passes away to the great sorrow of his sisters Martha and Mary. Most who have heard this story are familiar with the angst of the sisters that Jesus had not responded immediately and come to the aid of Lazarus by healing him of his illness as he had so many others. Instead Jesus comes to them after Lazarus has lain dead for four days and in another show of his power Jesus calls to Lazarus and commands him to "come forth." Lazarus arises at the command with the dressings he was wrapped in and Jesus instructs those watching to unbind him and let him go. For most, this story is another demonstration of the power Jesus commanded; but the story is more than that. It demonstrates the power he said we all have as well when we become *like* him. The point I want to make, however, corresponds to what happened after Lazarus was raised from the dead. The verses that follow tell us that many of those who observed what unfolded became believers, but also that some of them went to the Pharisees, the ruling class at the time, and told them what Jesus had done. The story continues with the Chief Priests and Pharisees gathering to discuss what to do about Jesus. Here is what they consider: "If we let him thus alone, all men will believe on him; and the Romans shall come and take away both our place and nation." The story continues from that point on with the Chief Priests and Pharisees conspiring to put Jesus to death. This is an extreme act of ego that has no comparison! *Destroy the doer of these great acts!* Even by their own institutional rules, the acts of Jesus were great and good yet see how insidious and fearful ego is of losing its identity within the reality it creates? In essence the Chief Priests and Pharisees are concluding that "He is so good that he threatens us and the egotistical institutions we have created to uphold us. This cannot stand!"

This is a classic example of how insidious the egocentric devices of men can be. Individually and institutionally, the Chief Priests and Pharisees recognized the greatness of Jesus and acknowledged his power to perform miracles, including an apparent command over death, and yet they could not abide it. Never is it written that they have any interest in trying to understand where such power comes from, whether they could acquire it, or even if they could recruit Jesus to use it to their own advantage! Plain and simply *Jesus' goodness threatened their reality!* So deeply were they saturated in their institutional belief systems and individual ideology that the only thing they could come up with to deal with someone so profoundly good and powerful was to have him put to death! These were the most educated and wise people of their time and all their minds could understand was that Jesus posed such an enormous threat to their existing reality that they had to get rid of him for good. Not one of them proposed how awesome it would be to be able to do some of the things he did, nor even considered his instruction that each of them, like him, was capable of such miracles and acts of power.

This illustrates another biblical story of abject blindness and irrationality. The Israelites who wandered in the wilderness with Moses were attacked by poisonous serpents, causing the death of many. When the people came to Moses for a solution, he was commanded to place a serpent on a staff and raise it before the house of Israel and if the people would do nothing more than look at the serpent, their lives would be spared. One would think that anyone, even those who didn't believe they could be saved, would look at the serpent but in the story many would not! They refused to look and died from the bites of the attacking serpents. It's hard to say what the chatter in their minds must have been saying, but to find a reason to turn away from an act so simple is almost unbelievable! This after Moses had parted the Red Sea! Who would not look!! These are just examples of how rigid and reckless the egocentric mind of man can become. Ego literally paralyzes us within its reality and blinds us to everything else. The fear of its own death (of its identity) is so profound that it resorts to utter madness to prevent it!

There are some who read this who will ask, "But what about the church that Jesus built? Isn't that an institutionalized, egotistical construct?" The answer would be "yes" had Jesus built a church! He, however, did not construct a church. Building a church would have been contrary to his teachings. Jesus' message uniquely applies to *individuals* since it is through and because of individuals that any organization exists. In fact, no organization has ever existed that could entertain any idea of individual freedom and godliness while maintaining its own institutional construct or ideas. The two do not mix! Organizations always override individuality and reduce any uniqueness to a single institutional idea or identity. Organizations take precedence over any concept of individual identity or uniqueness. This was wholly inconsistent with anything Jesus taught. His message reached out to individuals and considered that all of us are gods with power such as what he demonstrated over and over and that in recognizing this in ourselves as well as others, no institution of any kind was necessary. More precisely, gods have no hierarchy, organizations, or government to regulate them. They do what they do without *infringement on* or *judgment of* anyone or anything else.

Jesus also recognized that acceptance of and surrender to institutional structures makes us lazy and frees us from accepting individual responsibility and accountability for our own creative acts. The success of any established religion is likely attributable to this type of surrender. Recall that ego always looks outward for answers. It is an easy life when we can pledge our allegiance to something outside the self and not have to worry about identification with our higher self. By surrendering to an organized belief system, we can yield all knowing and searching to that system. Organizations will even create a set of rules to judge others against so we need not do it. We need not listen to the inner voice because all that is needed to walk through life, albeit unconsciously, is handed to us by the institution we have enjoined ourselves to. All we do is give up our uniqueness and all is provided. The institution will even feed the ego and provide a measure of self esteem; as long as we do not fall outside of its all-encompassing guidelines, we will be recognized, accepted, and kept safe. Such recognition and acceptance is ego recognition and will never support inner knowing nor will it provide any of the answers to the deeper purposes of life.

The answer to the purpose of life cannot be given by the constructs of human invention, scholarly study, or institutional credentials. That is why such attempts to do so always digress into a discussion of a particular set of beliefs or supposed values, all of which are egotistical in nature and origin. Such answers cannot be known from a place of ego. Ego will never know no matter how hard it tries to provide answers through institutional means, constructs, or individual ideology and so, we must ask ourselves what things do we attach ourselves to that define us egotistically? Perhaps you see yourself as tough for having fought your way to a particular social standing, a proud underdog, as it were. Are you brilliant and highly degreed with honors and acclaim awarded from recognized institutions of higher learning? Does such acclaim and honor validate other things you have not accomplished or that you recognize as inadequacies in your life? What is it that you hold onto in your life that you believe is what anchors you to reality? Is it your job or position, the way you look, the house you live in, the car you drive, the people you know, the religious or spiritual beliefs you hold, or the places you've been? Maybe it is family status or genealogy, wealth, class, family name, or your own children and their accomplishments. What are your "talking points" or the things that you must reveal when you converse with others and how big or complex is the story you tell about yourself? What or where are your "buttons" that when pushed, throw you into a fit of anger, jealousy, sadness, glee, depression, or some other form of emotional outburst? What offends you? What rules for yourself and others do you use to judge the acts of others? What are the secrets that you guard and struggle to keep hidden from others and out of play for yourself? How far will you go to defend your status or place in the reality you consider so important? All of these and so many more things that we attach ourselves to, or indulge in, are the things the ego thrives on and needs to have position in the collective ego. All of these things require an ongoing internal conversation to be upheld and as long as we are caught up in the noise of that conversation, the inner knowing that is the domain of gods is hidden from us. The ego believes there is safety in numbers as well as in holding secrets. Believing in the safety of the collective or holding secrets is what blocks the *knowing* we are all capable of. We must find a way to silence the conversation so that inner knowing, indeed the god within, can find its way into the light and truly set us free of so many things that are of so little importance.

Quiet knowing needs no institutional dogma or structure to support it, nor does it need to prove anything with signs or miracles. It simply *is*. In the light of individual knowing, the collective is quieted also. The need to shout at this or that or to let the mind spin in endless conversation is no longer necessary as the quiet assurance from within seeks to bask in the light that only gods can know. In such light, the serpent withers and dies, and as it does so individually, it passes on collectively as well. *All* reason fails in the light of quiet knowing. In order to find life, we must lose our egotistical selves and in order to do so, we must learn to listen to the voice of God who dwells within each of us. The voice of God is the voice of stillness. Stillness speaks in a way we cannot comprehend or describe using normal language but when it speaks, it is loud and clear. It is simply a knowing that permeates every part of our being and it is certain, profound, and without argument. In order to hear its voice, however, we must be still. That is the only way stillness can find us and impart the knowing we all have within.

Stillness speaks and its message is "Be still and know that I am God." *Be still and know that you are god!!*

Chapter 5

The Unconscious Life

The Dreamer and the Dreamed

For many of us, life as we now know it is the dream, a dream in the sense that who we really are is unknown to us and sleeps soundly amidst the noise, hustle and bustle of everyday life, and egocentric conversation. Occasionally, as we dream, our level of consciousness is raised to a level of awareness that reminds us, as we sleep, that we are asleep. That something or someone long forgotten is there beneath the noise, quiet and calm, but ever present and sometimes only aware as through a fog or mist. Occasionally, we sense another self and wish we could know it in a way that we know *other* things in our typical *dream world.*

We are often reminded that we are something else, completely different from that which we manifest in the dream. At times, it is as if the part of us that is asleep and the part that is the dream become simultaneously and vaguely aware of the other's existence, but also know that being in the presence of the other is intolerable. It is a parallel awareness that is often fleeting, but nonetheless powerful and jarring to all of our senses. At these times, we become thoughtful and contemplative and wonder "Who Am I?", or we may ask other deep questions such as "Where did I come from?" and "Where am I going?" It is almost as if the sudden awareness of that sleeping self is a *haunting*, a calling out from another part of ourselves that is eerily familiar but distant and unknown as well.

The feeling is not unlike *déjà vu*. Sometimes we may ask, "What was that?" We may become quiet and subdued and contemplative as we try to put into our own three-dimensional terms what we know, *but don't know!* Our contemplation may take us back through our history to recapitulate defining events in our lives that shaped us but drain us of our energy. Some of those past memories may trigger sorrow, joy, sadness, happiness or any number of other emotions or feelings that seem to cause us to retract into another place of meaning, discovery, and knowing that we struggle to understand. "Where did I go?" we may ask as we try to bring forward into present time that seemingly lost soul we thought we knew and actually did know sometime before. Locked inside that knowing, we struggle to identify *who* it was that was hidden away and forgotten, only to be thought of in these rarest of moments when, for whatever reason, the dreamer tries to awaken from that deep *unknowing* sleep.

It is as if the dreamer dreams and the dreams themselves live. They do, in fact, seem so real that we are lost to the illusion on display before us and rarely do we ever escape it. Life for most of us *is* the dream of one who fell asleep long, long ago, perhaps as children. The process of falling asleep begins at birth when everyone in our newly awakened life takes on the responsibility of convincing us that what they see is all that is there. Every institution we are exposed to in life from our birth to our death is the magic dust that keeps us asleep.

What we call 'reality' really is the illusion, the dream, the life played out as the dreamer sleeps. The dreamer, aware of the *other* reality being played out but frozen in the dream, tries to awaken or call out as if to cry, "Stop! That is the dream. True reality can only appear when I awaken. I am the only way to true reality and the answers you seek. Be still and you will find me, for I am always here" the voice of the dreamer whispers. Sometimes we almost awaken and know that we have been dreaming and our hearts fill with a wanderlust and exhilaration as we catch a glimpse of the true reality outside the dream. We struggle inside the dream to awaken fully to this distant knowing, long ago tucked away in the bright lights of the illusion we now experience.

Sadly, for most of us, the dream overwhelms the dreamer because the language of the dreamer cannot be understood in the language of the dream. The dream is action and drama, movement and suspense. The dreamer is still and quiet and falls again and again back into the deep sleep where the dream lies safe and protected from any onslaught of *true reality*.

It really is like watching a movie. The events are unreal but we attach ourselves to them emotionally as if they were. We let ourselves get drawn into the action as if we were really a part of the fictional events taking place. So lost in the movie do we become that we lose all awareness that we are sitting in a theater watching unreal events as if they were real, believing they are real!

We have coined new terminology that accepts *non-reality* as good enough to be reality. We call it 'virtual reality.' Virtual reality might be thought of as *the reality of non-reality*, if that could possibly make any sense. Think about non-reality becoming *more* real. As *non-reality* becomes more real, *reality* becomes less real. The less real *reality* becomes, the more difficult finding and knowing the dreamer becomes. In other words, virtual reality is "the dream becoming the dreamed." *There is no longer a dreamer!*

The language already exists that makes the ego lord over all. It is the language that states, "We can feed you non-reality that is so real, you have no need for *real* reality". That is the language of ego serving every need of man to the exclusion of an inner knowing of the *I am* that dreams it all. Wake up, dreamer, and know thyself!

The unconscious life is the life of the dreamer never waking from the dream. It is succumbing to the actual dream – the illusion that plays out as the life we live. Somehow, we must awaken from the sleep that dreams the dream we accept as reality, for everything we see or perceive as the dreamer sleeps is illusion. All of it is illusion if not perceived by the awakened dreamer, the *I am,* that is one with all things great and small. The dreamer is he, who in those brief moments of insight or awakening, is the non identity we seek that is interconnected to everything in existence. Sometimes our reckoning with this insight is so overwhelming that we lose all sense of our identity and we simply breathe in all of life and our oneness with it. We no longer see *it* as something that lies before us; rather, *we are it and it is us!* We are *quickened,* as it were, and the dreamer outside the dream is aware of nothing but oneness with all that is—the unidentifiable *I Am t*hat always is revealed to our knowing! Not our language but our true inner knowing, the knowing that cannot be known at the physical sense level other than a burst of insight and exhilaration we feel all over.

Gods have no identity, other than the ones we give them, and neither should we since we, too, are gods. Our identities, which we are so attached to, tie us to the dream and give us place within it, adding to the virtual drama being played out day in and day out.

When Moses was commanded to lead the Israelites out of Egypt, he asked God, "Who should I tell them has sent me?" to which God replied "Tell them *I am* has sent you." Who is the *"I Am"* God was speaking of that would be recognizable to the house of Israel? How do we identify with *"I Am"* when we are specifically looking for something to identify ourselves with? *"I Am"* is not an identity but a state of being. It is not a *who* but a *what!*

Moses asked for an identity and he received a *state of being* instead. *"I am* has sent you." *Gods do not need an identity.* Look at the different identities and ways we have tried to describe God through the ages. We say He is all knowing, mysterious, everywhere and nowhere, all powerful, the same yesterday, today and forever, so small He can dwell in your heart and so large He fills the universe, mindful of the least of these, but vengeful and jealous, kind and full of grace, perfect.

All of these descriptive terms are an *unidentifiable* way of identifying someone or something, and yet God in answering Moses' inquiry, rather than giving him an identifiable name to use, provided a state of being. In reality, it is useless to try to identify God as anything outside of *I Am*. Gods simply *are* and when you strip away the illusion of ego and still the chattering mind, so are we. So, to the unidentified, nothing need be identifiable. It simply is a part of one universal and infinite *I am*, none greater than or less than. All things sharing a common *I am*-ness that makes all things, including us, are equal. We are, as is everything, infinite awareness. Simply *I am that I am*. We are existence!

When we awaken and begin living that reality, the illusion we once lived, the dream recedes into quiet background that only serves to give us a context with those who never reach the same awareness. In other words, we know the reality in which they live, and can access them, live with them in every way, even though we have moved beyond that reality. In this way, we can exist in a reality we know does not exist as anything other than an illusion or the dreams of many dreamers. It is "being in the world but not of it."

Once we reach this state of being or awareness, *things* and *people* as we once knew them no longer need identification. Histories and stories are no longer necessary. Identifiers of any kind are no longer adequate in describing anything nor are they necessary. All the baggage of knowing *differences, placements, and time lines* are no longer important and are no longer necessary as we perceive that everything in existence is energy radiating in every direction and mingling with our own. Our new perception, or new seeing, takes on beauty that no three- dimensional sensing can comprehend.

Rare is the dreamer who wakes from the dream, and yet it is from the dream we must awaken in order to know the "I Am" within. That is where our true power lies and all the mysteries of heaven and earth come from that place, a place deep within. We are all gods, but for most of us, God sleeps. The noise of ego keeps the divine self at bay and our *virtual reasoning* convinces us over and over again that the illusion we all live in is the reality. All of our institutions support that and convince us ever more that the *dream* is anything but a dream.

We are gods and we all somehow know it when we awaken from the dream state most of us dwell in. Recognition of our godlike nature will never happen while we remain trapped in the illusion of our dreamlike state. The projection of life, the illusion we have accepted through years of egocentric conditioning, lacks the ability to comprehend the true power we all possess. We will never know it living the illusion and watching what most of us call 'life' play itself out. After all it is only a dream!

How do we know we are in the dream? The dream or illusion is finite. *Anything upon which we put finite limits is illusion!* That which is finite has a beginning and an ending and carries a finite description as to what it is in three dimensional terms. Ego needs finality-a right or wrong or absolute answers to questions that have no answers when speaking of the infinite. When we look out at anything and see only what we have been conditioned to see we can describe it in very finite terms. In other words "the tree is a tree" or more specifically "the tree is an oak tree." Illusion comes with description and details-identifiers that make it perceptible in our three dimensional terms and limited to that description.

Life, true life, is infinite. Without beginning or ending. It is so much more vast than any dream. In fact, in three dimensional terms, it is incomprehensible. It can only be comprehended through the eyes of the dreamer who is typically asleep-unconscious to what is really going on around him. The inner self, the dreamer, as it were, has the eyes to see but will rarely see. Most dreamers sleep comfortably, some fitfully, in the noise of illusion and the egoic drama that plays on and on. The non-identity, the *I Am*, always still, always quiet awaits the dreamer to become again as a child and awaken anew into the fullness of life and the acceptance of all that is! Children know this until we who sleep put them to sleep making them a part of the same dream we dream only now we have added more dreamers to the virtual reality we accept as reality.

Chapter 6

Personal History

There is a saying often quoted: "Those who fail to learn from history are bound to repeat its mistakes." We refer to this while standing in the rubble of numerous *repeated* mistakes. Perhaps we should forget history, or at least our personal history, since the real tendency is to not only repeat it but also to perpetuate it. It is the law of attraction at work. That which we focus on, we attract. Actually, it is more accurate to say, that which we focus on, we *create*. If we are continuously stuck in a realm of thinking that asks "Why me?" we are forever creating the circumstances around which this questioning occurs, and it will not end until we change the question.

The question can only change when our thinking changes. If our thoughts are conceived and then analyzed (thought about) from a historical premise we believe to be negative, we are doing nothing more than creating more of the negative. Even if we think our thoughts are constructive and conceived with a newly positive attitude, if they are derived from that historical pool, we will create only more of the same. History should be left where it is, in the past, especially as it relates to our own creative processes. *Now* is all there is and is the only point in time or space where we have total creative control and the ability to free ourselves from the junk of past thinking. The past, or history, has no reality other than that which we give it in our mind, in our thinking. Our ability to reincarnate our history and pull it forward into our present along with all the feelings and emotions we experienced is the part of the creative process that keeps us locked in with what we already have or are.

The *self*, as we call it, is inextricably tied to the description of the world as we view it. It might even be said that our view of self is a description within a description we have come to accept and believe because this is what we have heard all of our lives.

Again, we allow ourselves to be described by that over which we have no control, in other words our personal history. Not only is personal history the construct that makes up our lives as events and happenings, both as observer and player, but also as the observed. Very little of what we have done or do throughout our lives has been done in secret where no judging eye observed our actions, including our own. It is difficult to go anywhere or do anything without such observation, and it starts from the very moment of birth. We are cuddled and hugged and smiled at, laughed at from the very first looks or sounds we make, and on it goes. We are conditioned at birth and throughout the rest of our lives to look for and find approval or avoid non-approval. We are taught that our value, our measure of goodness or badness, is a condition of the amount of approval we can get for our actions while under some watchful but scrutinizing eye.

It is not wrong to observe or to be observed. In fact, it is impossible not to do, but the judgment of the observer coupled with the feeling of the observed attaches us to each other in an unhealthy way. It places us in the position of needing or seeking the approval or avoiding the non-approval of someone outside ourselves.

Man seeks onlookers or outside observers for acceptance and approval. Some even call self-confidence the measure of approval or acceptance people have attained in a given situation. Credentials have become extremely important in identifying or labeling our many accomplishments so that other observers may instantaneously judge us or place us on a scale that measures us based on whatever criteria we deem important enough to judge by at the time.

We are observers but we observe through the lens of judgments we have learned throughout our lives. In our personal description of the world, accomplishments and credentials are the yardstick we use to determine the level of clarity, the lens we use to look through. The greater the accomplishment as viewed by the world, the clearer the lens. This then becomes an endless game of seeking accomplishment for the sake of accomplishment. Approval becomes a game of recognition we continuously seek out because the reality of our world looks to this as the measure of man.

Self-confidence is not truly self-confidence if it is in any way tied to outside observers or observation in any form whatsoever. It is not a place of humbleness to feel inferior or superior to another. Gods see themselves as completely apart from everyone and from all things. They are neutral with no distinctions of any kind. We are all in this together, regardless of our place in a man-made observatory or so-called pecking order. In the end, we all come together, good or bad, great or small, and nothing we have done or will do matters in terms of three-dimensional importance. As gods, we are inseparably connected to infinity. Infinity? In this reality, we are connected to the descriptions of other men, to the things we have accepted as good or bad but all of it is nothing when compared to the infinite splendor we really have around us and which we are a part of.

Where does our description of the world fit in with a description that is truly infinite? Think about it—all of our accomplishments, or the accomplishments of anyone's idea of the greatest human to have ever lived, in relationship to *infinity!*

Jesus related Himself to infinity: "I and my Father are one." The same. No difference now or ever. Even at age 12, He was about his Father's business and He was about it in spite of those "observers" who marveled at His wisdom. His Father's business would continue even without the approval of others. He was one with His Father, as are all of us. His purpose was in no way connected to any description of the current conditions or situation of the times. He was supremely confident and knew His *self* as no other. He never bought into the folly of the learned or credentialed men of that time. Everyone, even everything, was equal, to the point that He mingled with the unclean, as they were described by the *observers* of that time. There simply was no unclean thing in His reality!

As long as we hold to our current description of the world, we are bound to its judgments of us. We will never see beyond it, rise above it, and never see the infinite splendor of the world as gods see it.

Our personal history is what ultimately forms the criteria by which we judge ourselves, as well as the picture that is painted for others to judge us by. It is the illustrations we paint and present to the world that we want others to see regardless of whether it is an accurate illustration or not. The painting is never really completed as we continuously look for substantiation and better ways to present how we want the world to see us. It is our own little game of "hide and seek" that hides as much as possible, the more others seek our true history. We weave our webs in such a complex fashion that it becomes impossible to untangle ourselves from them and for what? To sell an image that must look good in this reality when none of it matters compared to our infinite natures? The historical attachments we make in this life are anchors that continuously pull on us and drain us of vital energy needed for the present moment. It is not that we have to forsake our families, friends, or experiences. We must, however, detach ourselves from the identity we create with those historical people and events. They are not what we are now unless we make them a part of it. As hard as it sounds, the past does not exist. The anxiety we feel from a controlling parent, the fear of an abusive relative, our phobias and emotional aches and pains only have control in the present because we allow it by bringing them forward into our awareness. It need not be that way. Letting go of our personal history removes the mystery and effort we put ourselves through to create the image of who we want to project to the world. It is unimportant how others view us, and when we let go of the need to have others view us in a particular way, we take back our energy and put it into our present reality which is the only place it does any good anyway. The more people we entangle in our history, the harder it is for us to let it go because everyone who knows our history reminds us of it every time they see or talk to us. It is like being wrapped up in the tentacles of an octopus. When we peel one tentacle off it latches on with another.

It should not matter what others think or say about us. It is their right to think whatever they want, but their idea of us should not be predicated on any historical identities we have provided them with. The nature of our conditioning is to have others fuel our stories while we fuel theirs. We do this by giving attention to the historical identities they have carried forward into the now and we look for them to give us equal time for our historical identity. Sometimes it can even become a game of "one up-man-ship," in that we try to outdo the stories of others with the telling of our own. We can watch this interaction play out as individuals vie for a space in conversation with others to jump in and tell their tale. It is as if they are only listening superficially so they can jump in at the perfect time. No real attention is given to the individual telling their tale and so a sort of "cat and mouse" game of who has the better story ensues. It seems that the notion that someone will listen to our story telling is the energy we need to fuel our identity even though our listeners are really only concerned about their own. This, too, has become part of the illusion we live in. The more individuals we can pull into our web of identity and who will carry the identity our history has created, the more difficult it is for us to overcome that identity and to connect with the truly mysterious individual we are. Likewise, the more we reveal our history and tie our emotional and psychological selves to it, the further we drive our godlike nature into to obscurity and the more difficult it is to connect to the truly wondrous beings we are. Making your personal history available for everyone to see allows them to either take you for granted or to boost your ego, and it is difficult to break free of their conceived ideas of us because once they know our story they will constantly remind us of it. In either case, it is an outward, artificial view that makes you feel good or bad about yourself but does nothing to extol what you really are. Being taken for granted in egotistical terms is very difficult to deal with, and yet we create the opportunity for others to take us for granted by putting our history in front of them to judge us one way or another. True personal freedom lies in not having a personal history that others can judge and remind us of every time they see us.

Having no personal history surrounds us in mystery and while that won't stop others on the outside from making judgments about us, we are unaffected because there is no way they can know what really lies within and what lies within us is so much more than anything they can uphold. We cannot be taken for granted because all personal context, and therefore any criteria for judging us, is removed. We become *mystery* and "everyone loves a mystery!" When you consider your unique godlike nature, no one really knows you anyway and the illusion of our personal history is a culmination of events, circumstances, and emotions that mask the real you that truly is mysterious and wonderful beyond any historical description we can devise. We are so much more than any limiting historical perspective we can create and it is our reliance on it that prevents us from seeing anything beyond it.

Our current reality seems to be desperate for historical context for everyone and everything. It is nearly impossible to have a conversation that does not thrust us backward in time. We analyze and rate past experiences in the context of the present and repeat and repeat our stories so that it is difficult to ever see beyond it. We draw energy from others as they do from us.

The quandary of this current reality is that all the things that go into it that we have dragged forward from our past makes it difficult to see anything other than *it*. Our reality is a construction of the collective thoughts, ideas, and historical perspectives we have been conditioned over and over again to accept and believe to be true and our lives play out that reality every minute. Our history is the proof of our *current* playing out and the more attached to it we are, the more difficult it is to break free of the things we accept and believe because of it. Freeing ourselves of the emotional conditioning we believe is what makes us who we are is the only way we will ever be able to comprehend our true greatness and our own unique and divine natures.

We have control over our histories but only when we come to realize that all control comes out of our present moments. We may not be able to go back in time and change anything that happened, but in the present moment, we have complete control over any suffering or damage we think it has caused us. We are not defined by anything that has happened in the past nor are we what our current reality defines us as. In reality, we are beyond anything we conceive in this reality. We are only defined by what we *accept* to be true and if we pull historical identities into the present and allow them to have place in us, we consequently give them life. The only identity we need to have is the one that comprehends its own divine nature and its place in the eternities. *Now* is the only place or time in the universe where such comprehension exists.

Chapter 7

The Language of History

I am the same yesterday, today, and forever. What was, "is." What will be, "is." "All is."

Language is the device we have created to communicate abstract ideas, concepts, and collective knowing to others within this three-dimensional reality we exist in. Language, or our ability to communicate verbally with each other in a highly complex way, is one of the things that distinguishes us from many other life forms we know on this planet. Everything we take in through our five physical senses is translated in words that provide conscious meaning and gives us a description of the world as we perceive it to be. Words are used to catalogue our knowing and to place that knowing in historical, scientific or religious context so that we always have a point of reference from which to discern what we claim to know. Words, however, just as learning, flow chronologically which put them into a linear form that requires they be added to and carried forward. Words are used to teach ongoing generations but teaching or learning, as a process, focuses our attention on the process itself to the exclusion of the *learned*, confining us to so very little that is actually going on around us all the time. There is very little place in our learning processes to open us up to the incredible things going on around us that we cannot explain in our various languages. Scientifically we know that we are limited to the amount of input we as physical beings are capable of comprehending, yet we also know that outside the things we can comprehend there is so much more. Some of us become aware of those, seemingly, invisible things through others means, as has been discussed before. Teachers as well as teachings come in many forms. We are learning and continue to learn throughout our lives but for many, the target of learning is focused on very specific process types of knowledge that will fulfill specific requirements of a career or vocation. The nature of our reality is that happiness comes through an improvement of our conditions. As such, higher education prepares us for greater monetary rewards and status inside the institutions and businesses that require a particular expertise. As a result of our process enhancement, we are able to maintain a higher "quality of life" as it is called but in so doing we often overlook all the other teachers and great lessons in life that are before us every day. Our drive to better ourselves in the illusion not only contributes more and more to the illusion, but it also blinds us ever more to true reality. The more expression we seek to find in the illusion, the harder it becomes to know reality. Our world suffers from this lack of knowing true reality and we sink deeper as we all strive to find place in the illusion. Our greatest teachers are not institutional teachers nor does our greatest learning take place inside institutions we call "places of higher learning." Our greatest learning comes from that which we cannot see or comprehend in terms of our known languages. Our greatest teacher is literally the god within that has awareness of things not comprehensible in our three-dimensional reality. It is a sad paradox. The world as we know it expects us not only to learn by embracing the illusion of our current existence, but also to seek specific knowledge that will make our place within it comfortable and acceptable to all others, most of whom are also caught up in the illusion.

The words we express as we endeavor to share our knowledge also lock us into one-dimensional aspects of the language. In other words, our knowledge is connected to our history and it gets articulated in a way that is descriptive only in terms of that language. Language is only useful in three-dimensional terms and it is used to reinforce what we think we know or should know about our three-dimensional reality. We often use terms such as "in my opinion" or "my thoughts on it are," etc. Such expressions are part of the limited reality, the confinement, the illusion creates around us and in us. They are our attempt to describe in three-dimensional terms why we think what we think or why we believe what we believe. We must be careful with the words, opinions, and thoughts we express, think to ourselves, or share with others as they lock us into a train of motion that tracks only one direction and leads only to one destination. That destination is a very narrow view of what is really going on in our reality. Language is a finite medium of expression that reinforces constantly what we believe ourselves to be in three-dimensional reality. It is inadequate for describing the gods that we are and the infinite wonder we exist in and are innately a part of. Language, coupled with our need to know everything, in ways that are explainable three-dimensionally, constricts us from a greater possibility of knowing far beyond anything we currently understand or think we know.

Ultimately we talk too much!! We as curious beings are chronically engaged in describing everything in three-dimensional terms that are easy for us, and hopefully for others, to understand and so we think and talk constantly about everything that comes into the view of our senses. We literally talk about our world as we believe it to be and through such talking, we convince ourselves that what we are talking about is the way it is. Most of us can't turn the talking off and so everything that is in our purview is constantly being reinforced, rehashed, re-analyzed, and restructured to fit into our view of the world. The chatter is so incessant that we almost never hear God or *who we really are!!* We tend to be so insistent on understanding everything in three-dimensional terms that it becomes a serious stumbling block to what our true purposes in life are. Our true purpose in life is to know God! In other words, our lifelong intention is to know the higher form of existence we truly are. God does not exist out there somewhere in the heavens, as it were; rather, *our higher form of existence is the god we seek.* We are gods and our thinking and talking takes us further from the divine because thinking and talking can only make sense of three-dimensional things. Our purpose in life, simply stated, is to live life without judgments of any kind and in a reality of non judgment all things are equal! We live to appreciate all that is and to simply appreciate the wondrousness of being in a physical reality that allows us to feel everything without judgment and simply enjoy it all!! Our egotistical need to define everything and to give expression to even those things we cannot understand dilutes the incredible beauty of the reality we see and are a part of. Finding a description of everything that uniquely defines things in three-dimensional terms limits us to that unique description, and it is our description of the world that prevents us from seeing anything beyond it! The language of man is limited and can only define things in a finite way. Another language must be used when we look beyond the finite to the infinite. The language of gods, the language of energy, is only found in the silence we create by shutting off the thinking mind.

When we stop talking to ourselves, we open ourselves to the vaults of eternity and the understanding of men which can only be understood three-dimensionally, gives way to knowing that is not of this world but of the infinity of which *it* is only a part. The language of infinity is silence and the sweetness of knowing, as the gods know, is simply known. There is no describing it in three-dimensional terms, and thus there is no reason for talking and explanation. Metaphorically, we need to *see with our ears* and to *hear with our eyes* that which can only come from an unspoken language we all know but have simply drowned out in the language of everyday life. *The greater part of understanding is that which cannot be comprehended or explained by the languages we speak!* When we stop talking to ourselves and silence the noise of language and thinking, we become the receptors of understanding and knowing that descends upon us from the vast stores of the universe from which there is no beginning or end.

We have heard it said that "We are all one." We as a species are all one. We are, however, also one with all things, not just the human family, but everything in existence from the lowly rock to the mountains, rivers, stars, and galaxies. We are literally a part of everything we see and don't see in this universe. We are inextricably connected at a deep level to all that is, was, or will ever be. In fact, to say that we are connected to all that was, is, or will be is a great example of the limitation of our languages. Past and future do not exist and cannot be a part of the *now* that we find ourselves in! We carry the past with us in our minds and the future we fantasize about but they are non existent and our language is incapable of grasping that concept. Instead, we devise languages that give them meaning and place in our limited understanding and we are forever trying to reconcile non existence with existence. They are both without meaning except to the mind that has quieted itself and the inner god who knows all things on some other level that cannot be put into to the words of language as we know it. Our existence is truly profound when we give up viewing it in the confinement of our own illusions that are constantly reinforced by our talking, thinking, and language. Sometimes in the quiet stillness of the mind, all that is simply *is* and that is all the knowing we need. *At the energetic level everything just is!*

The God of the Old and New Testaments stated, "I am the same yesterday, today and forever." It might be better said, "I am yesterday, today, and forever." There is no distinction between past, present, and future in the realm of knowing quiet, distilled truth; all of us at one time or another have felt the peace that comes in that knowing. It settles upon us like mist and completely engulfs our mind and soul with an awareness that is unexplainable. Space and time lose their meaning at such times. Knowing is the most sublime dimension and it operates outside space and time as our language has described it. Knowing is the only place gods could ever make the statement that they are yesterday, today, and forever because in such a place time and space have no bounds. They don't exist. Three-dimensional physics hold no ties to the infinite possibilities of knowing.

In the realm of gods there is no language of time or space. There isn't a language of understanding that wrests our thinking and talking from an endless pursuit to comprehend everything three-dimensionally. Gods know all things exist inside the present moment and whether we judge those things good or evil is of no consequence in infinity. The space between the past and now or the future and now is nothing more than shadows. These are shadows of things we create and put there to fill a void that does not exist in infinity and is of our own making. There is no life past or life future. It all is happening now, in the present and we don't need to understand it! We don't need a historical context or three-dimensional perspective. The energy of life exists always and has never been disconnected in any way to time past or time future. There are no voids in space or time! The energy of life is always teeming and present; it permeates every construct we have created to define it in three-dimensional terms. *Energy is everywhere and energy is life!!* All that we think we were or will be is all happening now and only in this *now* can we know what gods know!! In this present moment, where the confines of space and time cease to exist, we as ageless existence, witness our oneness with it. It cannot be comprehended nor need it be. Our oneness with it transcends comprehension of the mind and simply makes us *it!*

We are the good that we love, the evil we hate, the darkness we fear, the light that gives hope. We are all things, people, places we imagine or cannot imagine. We are all thoughts and forms and are endowed with power to create the good we cherish or the evil we despise in this existence. We are the beauty that loves and the ugliness that hates. We are the *then*, the *now*, and the *yet to be* simultaneously in a never-ending, timeless sea of infinite life. We are receptors of every form of energy that surrounds us continuously and endlessly and while we do not have a language in this reality that can accurately describe everything that is going on around us, we do have a language, not of words and expressions, that communicates to us clearly that we are a part with everything in the universe!! We are being spoken to by infinity every single moment of our lives and all we need to do is stop, be still, and listen; in waves of indescribable beauty it pours into us.

The spectrum of time and space leaves us wondering about the "how" of all things. Our egocentric minds want to know order, both in terms of chronology for time and in terms of placement for space, in the reality we have created. We crave this knowing and want our language to describe it to us so we understand in relationship to our reality.

Instead of feeling the wonder of existence and our oneness with it, we want to define it, thus diluting it in finite reason and dogmatic conjecture. We search for definitions and descriptions where none are needed nor will we ever be able to develop a language that could ever give adequate meaning to the spectacle of this infinite universe we are all a part of. We must leave the norms we have come to accept and step outside time and space to ever be able to know as the gods all the mysteries we seek to know and describe. Leaving the spectrum of time and space leaves us in absolute awe of everything. Good is evil and evil is good. It *all* just is. We breathe all of it in and embrace it as what we are, without judgment and without question, with no historical context or analysis of any kind. There is only acceptance and love, not the love that ties us to anyone or anything, but the pure love that holds no boundary. No limits. No emotion. Energetic love has no emotion and exists in all things, at all times, and in all places.

We have no words, no thoughts, no thinking. Ego has blended into everything else and all struggles have ceased. We have no arguments. The existence of every act, thought, or thing is us as we are it.

Existence fills our bodies as our bodies fill existence. All that is, is known to us because we are the knowing. The seeker no longer seeks that which is not understood. Knowing requires no understanding. "All is." We are the "all" that "is." Knowing simply rests upon us and it requires no words or expressions or thoughts or thinking to give it place in our existence. It fills us with wonder and awe that has no expression. In the quietness of mind, *knowing* finds a place where it instills itself and in that instant we know God, for He is us and we are Him.

"Be still and know the knowing." "You are god and in stillness He will find you."

Chapter 8

Awareness of Awareness

My thoughts are not your thoughts

Awareness is perhaps one of the great mysteries of the current illusion we all exist in. Most would see it as something common as we all see generally the same things that everyone else does and so it is easy to categorize our awareness as *not unusual*. It is analogous to the often repeated admonition to use "common sense." Common sense is only common when we see something as common and expect everyone else to agree. Everyone sees things slightly differently than everyone else but in the case of awareness it is almost always skewed by the eyes we have been conditioned to see through. Those eyes are our perceptual filters and are the result of a lifetime of conditioning we carry forward with us from the time of our birth to the present. Every aspect of our lives becomes a part of the lens our awareness will see through. The process of awareness is truly a unique and individual experience since no two of us are alike, nor have we had the same life experience. Simply stated, one man's *awareness* is not another's and because my awareness is not the same as your awareness, we now have the basis for judging.

Science would describe awareness as only that which we can take in through our physical senses. Yet all of us, at one time or another, have had profound moments of knowing or awareness that we have no idea where they came from but all the same, we know them as surely as if we had read about them in the latest scientific journal. Why do some *insights* come in such a way and why do they come to some more readily than to others? We may never know why they come seemingly out of nowhere the way they do and that is really not important. What is important is that this type of knowing is not on the spectrum of scientific knowing that requires everything to be known through the five physical senses. It is a different type of knowing that comes from some other sensing, undetectable to the physical senses. There are people who seem to be able to tap into this vast realm of other knowing, and at one time or another all of us have had similar flashes of insight and knowing. It is a level of awareness that is uncommon and while in our common state of awareness, we often view this other knowing as luck or the imaginings of a broken mind.

All we can say is that such knowing comes as a still, small voice that sometimes shakes us as if it were loud and thunderous, but it comes to us with such authority, clarity, and certainty that we are absolutely confident in its truth and our own awareness is heightened when we recognize it. It really does come from within. We know this because outside stimuli do not seem to be present, but the truth penetrates us in a deep way that cannot be known by the physical senses. It is as if we always knew it and in reality *we always have!* This sudden knowing is really nothing more than remembering. Again, we are infinite and have always existed in some form or another. We have always been part of the whole and continue to be in our current form.

What does it mean, however, that it comes from within? This is the great complexity of awareness because it defies the scientific construct that reality only occurs through that which we identify as the physical senses of sight, sound, smell, touch, and taste. We have been conditioned that if what we *know* does not come through one of these senses, we have cause to question or completely discount such knowing. In scientific terms, *knowing* what we know that has come to us from any other means other than that which we can see, touch, smell, taste, or hear is *not knowing*. There is a paradox however, in that knowing what we *know*, which has come to us through means other than the five senses (call it *not knowing*), makes *not knowing* a form of *knowing*. On an infinite scale, what is *not known* is vast and infinitely greater than all we claim to currently know. In fact, when we consider how vast the pool of *not knowing* is, we can begin to see that having access to that pool through means other than the physical senses might just be the best way of knowing and that we as humans, *gods really*, have a greater capacity to access knowing than through just our physical senses.

Looked at a different way, our physical senses are adapted to a space and time reality that at its own outer edges is confusing and uncertain. One of the great scientific discoveries of the last century, quantum theory or quantum mechanics, has shown that observable reality is affected by the observer. In other words, we as observers are not separate from the observed. What does that mean? It means the same as knowing by *not knowing*. It means that things that happen without an explanation acceptable to the physical senses can and, do happen and they do so without our understanding or any reasonable scientific explanations! More precisely, things happen that cannot be explained by what we have defined as the criteria for *knowing* — or the five senses.

In an existence of infinite possibilities, not only are all things possible but *we* are a part of every one of those possibilities. Quantum physics has shown this to be so. So how do we explain the unknowable? In the context of the five senses, we do not. We cannot. Physical senses cannot account for *uncertainty*; therefore, they cannot account for knowing what is *not known*. Uncertainty is what Einstein could not accept with the discovery of quantum physics and caused him to exclaim that "God does not play with dice." He would later concede that God does in fact play with dice but he had to overcome, as we all must, that literally anything is possible. Even that which we cannot imagine or make sense of in physical terms is possible.

Here is an example. Everything in the universe is energy. It is known that energy cannot be created or destroyed, but it can change form. We then are energy and have always been. Our thoughts are also energy and have always been. We know this about energy: it is endless and eternal. It has always been and always will be. Again, energy may change form but it always exists. So too, do we and our thoughts. We can detect thought through various means of instrumentation and see it as energy emitted through neural transmitters in the brain. Our thoughts are energy and as energy, have always existed. If *thoughts,* then, have always existed, as has everything else, is it not possible that thoughts that have not yet been defined or created by our physical senses exist somewhere and are available to be received or created outside of our physical knowing? Think about it.

If within the dimensions of time and space, time and space are endless and infinite, then *how can we possibly think that what we see, taste, smell, touch, or hear is all there is until we prove otherwise?*

The science of quantum physics and the Heisenberg uncertainty principle proves with *certainty* that *everything is*, but even more importantly, it proves that *anything* is. We cannot confine anything to our earthly existence and our physical senses only. In fact, it can be said that the answers to all questions exist before the questions are asked! Science rightly claims to only have discovered the laws of our universe which again, supports that there is a lot of *not known* yet to be known.

There cannot be a finite when everything is infinite. We have not even scratched the surface of creative possibilities that not only potentially exist, but exist already! We just don't know it yet!! As gods we have the ability to access this vast *not knowing* before it is realized there is a need for knowing it in three-dimensional terms! Such knowing is sometimes referred to as prophecy or *seeing* as seers were said to be able to do but it is, nonetheless, knowing.

This is the difference between knowing and not knowing. That which is not known dwarfs in comparison to that which is known. To the physical senses, the not known is unknowable and to those senses that might be true, but it does not mean that the not known is not real! All things are possible! Even what we, through our knowing, would say is impossible is possible! *The awareness of gods is an infinite awareness!*

In such a world of possibility, then, is it not also possible that we can know what is not known from time to time when new ideas, thoughts, or new awareness just seem to fall out of the sky for totally inexplicable reasons and we are simply left knowing what was previously not known? Many of us have felt this and it is often described as an "epiphany." Some have even called it "revelation." Regardless of what it is called, we are swept up in a wave of understanding and awareness that had completely escaped us previously. This too is a state of knowing.

It is our insistence on believing that we cannot know, that forms the basis for our chronic need to judge and drag such knowing through the filters of thinking and ego. Believing what we know we know and concluding that what we do not know is unknowable is what confines us to a very limited view of life, a view of what *really* is real and the wondrous spectacle going on all around us even while being invisible to us.

We have been conditioned to think that knowing must come to us serially or in some formal way that assumes, depending on our ability to comprehend, we are ready to learn and comprehend more. Our schools, colleges and universities are set up this way and we advance or increase in a structured, sequential way that has been determined to be best suited for us. This has also become a part of our awareness and our illusion. We must follow a prescribed educational pattern in order to advance to higher levels of learning. Some early Greek philosophers taught a reductionist view of the world and looked at all things in a very mechanical way, meaning that things can be explained by studying their integral parts. In the 1600s, Descartes would apply the philosophy of reductionism to scientific study to conclude that all mechanisms can be understood by breaking down, studying, and analyzing their component parts, and then putting the pieces together again so the "whole" could be understood. Many of the scientific discoveries of the last four hundred years, including classical mechanics, have been credited to the reductionist methods of reasoning. It is notable, however, that our educational processes have taken on a reductionist theme as well in that we start with the study and learning of small pieces of a larger system and over time work up to the whole. Ultimately it is believed that if we reduce things down to their smallest, base, individual components we will discover God, or in scientific terms, we will discover the theory of everything. Reductionism might be a great way to study the natural world but it will never be able to explain the supernatural world we all know exists. There is more to our perception of the world than what filters through the physical senses as we have discussed before. Our idea of education is also limiting in that it does not allow for any form of knowing outside the idea that it must come in a sequential way best prescribed by the authorities at that time.

In the support of our three-dimensional reality, "line upon line" as a way to educate and develop knowing is perhaps the best way to understand our three-dimensional reality; it is, however, a poor way to develop *other* knowing, which we have all experienced at one time or another and for no explainable or, reductionist, reason. Three-dimensional knowing causes us to question these other types of knowing that cannot be explained in reductionist terms and make judgments about what it is we have just experienced. This is where the filters of ego get turned on and what we believe has come to us through other perceptive awareness is questioned, debated, and scrutinized in a way that makes us doubt our ability to receive such things. Ego wants us to believe, as in Jesus' time, that if we have not satisfied the requirements of our sequential learning systems, we can't possibly have awareness greater than that level of learning. The fallacy of incremental knowing is that it requires previous sequential knowing that we believe must exist before we can absorb further knowing. It supposes that no other form of knowing is possible without appropriate conditioning that comes from previous sequential knowing. Our entire educational system is designed to support this sequential style of learning. The conditioning of this type of learning makes us question anything that didn't come in a prescribed way that is recognizable to the system.

This is what confounded the learned among the people in the time of Jesus because he came with "power and authority," but it was not of the established criteria they were conditioned to recognize. Their conditioning took years of scholarly study and training at the hands of masters. Yet even with their own criteria, members of the elite, powerful, and learned marveled at the power and authority by which Jesus taught and performed the miracles he did. Nothing in their system of credentials and identity could cope with such a person and so what did they do? They accused him of being a blasphemer and a charlatan. They literally could not see beyond their own criteria for what made power and authority and outside of their illusion, anyone else's power and authority could not be sanctioned! We have a similar awareness today and it locks us into a reality that is limited and unworthy of the gods that we are.

We are perceptual beings. We are also conditioned beings. Since our birth, our perceptive abilities are coupled with the conditioning that *others* such as relatives, have been conditioned to interpret and to project what they perceive *on to us*. In other words, we are told repeatedly what to identify from the very beginning of life to the point that our awareness is always shadowed by that conditioning. In essence we see what we are taught to see. Rarely are we *literally* taught that all things are possible and that we actually can see beyond what we have been taught. That is why culturally, ethnically, religiously, etc., we all seem to see and believe generally the same things within those confines, particularly within a given society. It is also the cause for division between societies of differing perceptions. It might be said that our perception of the world is also the world we project onto others. If we are raised in a particular society with religious, ethnic, or educational biases, we will tend to look at the world and judge everything according to those biases. We literally project our perception onto any society or individual outside our own. While the members of one society will generally believe the same things, their perception of other societies who do not perceive as they do can cause great, if not, catastrophic conflicts.

It is not that conditioned perception is wrong. In fact, it is absolutely right — wonderfully and profoundly descriptive and necessary to our existence in this three-dimensional reality we live in. The tree we love to sit under or swing from or the myriad of colors from a field of flowers fills our senses with incredible *sense* stimulation, wonder, and awe. It is all real before us and remarkable in every way. The problem with such conditioning is that while we sense the world around us, we only know what is there because that is what we have been told — *conditioned to believe* — is there. What is missing is that there is so much more that we don't see. We don't see it because we have only been conditioned to see what we see. That becomes the limit and narrow extent of our awareness!

Awareness is the state of *becoming* we all exist in but when our awareness is limited to the five physical senses, it is difficult to maintain a constant level of learning in three-dimensional terms. For some, three-dimensional awareness stalls out and we cannot seem to go beyond our current level and what we *know* and everything in our lives bears out and confirms this. We see this often as people struggle and work to reach a certain level in life, be it career, education, or whatever only to stop and never go beyond that point. It is as if reaching the objective is the pinnacle of their awareness and all desire to move beyond to even greater enlightenment is halted, thus wrenching our existing awareness tighter and tighter into place. Our perception, then, is the limit of our awareness and the projection of our reality. The kind of knowledge that comes to us through the physical senses by way of our educational institutions typically supports careers, vocations, and religious beliefs and while our three-dimensional learning may shed light on those deeper levels of knowing we seek to find, it will never lead to a knowledge of the deeper issues of life. Those can only be found within at a level of awareness that only gods know.

Three-dimensional awareness often loses its power to influence or alter our lives and we are left feeling empty and sometimes even betrayed. Some call it "being stuck," while others call it "burnout." It is one thing to be in a box and see out, but to be stuck inside a box we cannot get out of is to be stuck within the finite limitations of the box. Limited awareness is a box from which there is rarely any escape. We are bound to its boundaries with no hope of ever getting out. Some even become afraid to look out for fear their safe little world will crumble. Spirit broken, they keep themselves confined to these limits. Those who cannot look out beyond their own knowing and even accept that their awareness is limited are in a box from which escape is extremely difficult. It is not a physical box but it might as well be as the boundaries we have placed on the mind and soul are as rigid and strong as any wall before us.

Awareness is not something we all have just because we are physical beings who happen to have taken on human form. We are so much more than mere physical beings. We are infinite and energetic and have always existed and will always exist in some form. If we can accept our infinite and divine nature, then awareness becomes access to not only the known, *but the unknown and the unknowable!* It is comprehension of all things great and small *by all things great and small!* What is not comprehended in one form is comprehended in another, but every thing as well as anything *is* and we perceive according to our own unique awareness, an awareness that can be defined in human terms or in godly terms. If perceived as human then our awareness is finite and limited. If perceived as gods, then our awareness is infinite and eternal.

We are aware because we are gods and as gods, we are constantly looking for higher awareness. Our connection to all things is real and every fiber of our beings knows on some level that we are a part of something grand and wondrous beyond any three-dimensional level of awareness we find ourselves in. Our bodies and souls are aware of everything that goes on in our world, but our physical awareness only comprehends what it has been conditioned to comprehend. For most our awareness comes through only the physical senses but the more we awaken to the reality that what we see through physical sensing is just a blip on an infinite scale, the more likely our ability to comprehend a wider, more expansive view of everything increases.

Higher awareness does not come in the noise of physical sensing. Our bodies sense so much more than what the physical senses take in and there is so much more that is happening that does not register at those levels. Our bodies, which are instruments with an amazing ability to sense everything around us, even that which is invisible to the other senses, rarely senses it. Most of us have forgotten how to hear or see what the body hears or sees because our tuning has become coarse and dull. The noise of the physical senses makes it nearly impossible to hear anything beyond what they want us to be aware of.

There is a lot being done and said these days to "tune" up the body, but most of that tuning is focused on physical conditioning and strength. This is all good indeed, but the body is an instrument not unlike anyone of our other physical senses. It can sense things but at a much finer level than any of the five senses and therefore needs tuning as well. This is where stillness and meditation have been so effective in that they help to shut down the other mind, the voice of ego and thinking, thus letting the inner voice of god speak to us. The fine tuning of the body and the inner voice of god operate in the quiet. The input is so subtle and refined that those aspects of that higher level of knowing and awareness can only be comprehended when the noise of the other mind is quieted. This is the kind of bodily conditioning that wakes us up to this higher awareness, the awareness of gods.

Chapter 9

Expanding Awareness

The purposes of life can only be known in stillness, and that knowing is unique to every individual on the planet. In fact, it can only be known by the individual and it is so distinct and wondrous that it can only be known individually. The level of awareness each of us comes to in knowing our purpose is glorious and wonderful beyond anything that can be described in egocentric terms. It simply cannot be explained nor should it. It is infinite knowing. Language is finite and therefore cannot describe infinity.

What we can say is that infinite knowing permeates us in calmness and quiet and it will never look like anything we currently hold in our descriptive view of the world. You will not perceive it through any of the physical senses. You will know at a much deeper level, a cellular or quantum level, to use scientific terms. And it will be unexplainable in anything other than metaphorical terms, if that. No dogmatic beliefs or system of beliefs will ever be able to adequately explain this knowing, and yet the depth of clarity you possess will be unlike anything you have ever known.

No attempt will be made here to explain such mysteries. As no two people are the same, neither are there two like purposes of life. We come to it in our own way and time or we don't. It doesn't matter. There is a basic purpose to life and that is to simply live and be aware of every aspect of it in such a way that no judgments are made about all the things that happen to us or are going on in this life. Simply live life and breathe in as much of it as you can. Outside of that any purpose or quest is your own and can only be found by you! We all hold the key that unlocks the door to our own inner purpose. We all must unlock that door by ourselves. It should be of no concern to anyone how or when awareness comes to us or in what form it appears. What matters is that we condition ourselves to know it when or if it does come. This in and of itself could take a lifetime while for others it happens quickly and often. Conditioning the body to perceive what it is capable of sensing is one of the most important things we can do in this life for it is the only way we will ever be able to see beyond our current ability of insight and it is the sensing of gods we all possess. It is a higher order of awareness that cannot be known in the mind of man or through the five physical senses.

Every cell in our bodies has awareness. Each cell is a microcosm of life, unique and distinct, teeming with everything it needs to live, reproduce, protect, and defend itself and yet it is also a part of trillions of other cells cooperating in the creation of the macrocosm or form that we call our bodies. Each cell is separate but connected, and contains its own unique awareness coupled with the awareness of the whole, our bodies, as well. Each cell aware in its own way merges with all the others to become a huge sensor that is absorbing light from distant stars, energy from newly formed galaxies, and stimulation from every source possible in the universe. This is awareness that we all have right now and it is limitless. It is awareness that is not limited by the five physical senses, but rather just overwhelmed by them. Additionally, our lifetime of conditioning overrules this sensing with the idea that no such sensing can exist, but it does!

Each cell in our body is aware. It comprehends things in the micro world that get overshadowed by our awareness of the macro world. Our five sense awareness is powerful and yet it is limited in its ability to perceive outside of itself. This is because the ego sees through only those five senses. Since the ego has so much control over our perceptive input, it is difficult to get past any interpretation or description the ego ascribes to it. This is how ego and our three-dimensional form of thinking overrule other types of knowing.

Science has proven in so many ways the limitations of our five senses when compared to the literally billions and billions of inputs coming our way every second. We see only a certain range of colors in the light spectrum or smell or hear only partially; yet, the instrumentation to perceive so much more is all there. We have just forgotten how to use it.

Having this deeper awareness is an intuitional gift we all possess but in many cases don't use or have forgotten how to use. Intuition is what deciphers what individual cells sense at the micro level. Intuition detects small energetic impulses from every cell in our bodies. It literally is the *still small voice* within that is connected to every fiber of our being.

Ego has desensitized us to the intuitive responses we get from various inputs because the five senses are so loud and apparent. It's hard to dispute what filters through the five senses and because of their *obvious* nature, they are easy to accept as all there is. Most of us agree that at various times in our lives, we have had those intuitive moments or flashes of insight when something was about to happen, such as a death of a loved one or something about to fall or some impending danger, etc. We don't know where it came from or why, but we know with the kind of certainty that is inexplicable. Often we will talk ourselves out of these intuitive moments of knowing or convince ourselves that we're being superstitious or overly sensitive only to be amazed that *we knew it would happen* when it actually does. We may even tell ourselves we need to be more aware so we can receive these insights more often.

It is our thinking, rationalizing minds that block this gift we each have. We are all so conditioned to the loud, obvious voice that we think intuition must reach us this way as well. It doesn't and it won't and certainly not if ego ever has a look at it.

Comparing the five-sensory awareness to intuition is a lot like comparing classical mechanics to quantum mechanics. In the context of classical mechanics, sometimes thought of as the world of *big* things, everything seems to be understandable, ordered, and easily observed. It is a comfortable, relatively safe world because we can see it and comprehend it in five sensory terms. It is in the context of quantum mechanics or the world of the extremely small, or particles, that nothing is understandable or ordered as we know it. In fact, we know that at the quantum level, everything is uncertain and that any observation of things at this level makes it even more uncertain. That is, at the quantum level, observation affects outcome. How bizarre and yet eerily similar to the five senses awareness and intuition. The five sense awareness is the world of the big and obvious. Things are easily observed, perceived, and understood. Things fit neatly with our preconditioned description of the world we see everyday, and everything seems to be as we think it should be.

On the other hand, intuition is a perception of the very small, quiet, calm voice of stillness and energy. It is subtle yet real and we all seem to know it. Yet, like quantum uncertainty, intuition observed through the filter of the ego changes. Ego convinces us that something so abstract and completely "out of the blue" is not possible, or really is something like wishful thinking or whatever. *The observation of the ego on intuitive insight alters the insight.* Ego, looking through the lens of only the physical senses at something unexplainable, reasons that it cannot be and so works to convince us that what it cannot comprehend is not possible because it is *uncertain!*

Ego always seeks and argues for clarity – "show me the *how* and I can then be certain." Intuition always comes from certainty – "I simply know-no explanation needed." An example might look like this: An intuitive insight comes to you to quit your job. It is as clear as can be and in the instant you have it, you know it is right and you know it at the cellular level of your body. You are not even shocked by it. What happens? You run it through the ego and the ego has a hundred questions prefaced with the exclamation "Are you nuts? How are you going to do that? What about your bills? How will you take care of the children? What about insurance, benefits, etc. etc?" By the time the ego has leveled all the clarifying questions at the intuitive insight, it is no longer an insight but instead a passing fancy, a fluke, a pipe dream—and thank God that ego came in and rescued you from such an off-the-wall, frivolous act. Perhaps the job was draining your energy or maybe something better was waiting for just you, but you'll never know. The intuitive voice does not come with the clarity the ego seeks in terms of how and why. Intuition only comes in certainty. Short, sweet, and certain. At least that's all we hear. There always is a *how* with intuition but it is never given. It simply says, "Act! I'll take care of the details."

The voice of God, or intuition, never comes through the egocentric filter of humans. That is why we so rarely hear it or know it when we do hear it. Ego wants the voice to come in terms it knows, loud and clear and through the five physical senses. In other words "show us a sign!" Most of us who pray expect answers to come the same way. Recall that ego always wants clarity, description, the "how to," and proof to its supplications. While it acts subtly, it wants directness in answers to questions or when it senses the intuitive guidance within. Intuition, on the other hand, is the state of knowing. *Just knowing*. No reasons, no descriptions, no how's or whys. It may come in a form that is recognizable to the physical senses; for example, we may hear a voice but however it comes is inconsequential to the state of knowing that it came. We simply know at some deep unexplainable level and outside of the ego asking for explanation or offering doubt, it is as complete and sure as anything we have ever known. *Gods know.* They don't question knowing or let it be questioned by outside, thinking or egocentric forces. If action is required, they act.

Ego cares about outcomes and therefore looks for reasoning and *how* in everything it takes on. Intuition does not care about outcomes and only acts because something deep and profound has prompted it. Ego, because it cares causes worry and stress whereas intuition, if it is listened to, does not. Caring and worrying are the by-products of running everything through the filter of egocentric mind. Ego always wants to know how something is to be accomplished and is always predisposed to judging outcomes as good or bad; therefore, it must *care* about everything it approves the physical to do and worry about its effectiveness once the doing begins. Ego must care because it has overridden intuitive knowing with its own "how to." It must worry for the same reason.

In the realm of judgment, we reduce our own acts and those of others to a *self* imposed importance that cannot escape analysis and more judgment. Ego cannot let *acts* be just acts. It evaluates everything on a finite scale of good or evil. Ego must have choices because it is a finite entity and the world of finite things is the world of opposites. To accept infinity would be too much for ego and to do so would be its own end.

Intuition, on the other hand, only requires quiet acceptance and *will*, not caring or worry. Since intuition is knowing at another *sensory level*, it requires no analysis or judgment at any level. Intuition accepts the world of infinity and understands that things not comprehended at the three-dimensional level are real. Questioning such insights is unnecessary because intuition understands that all things are possible with gods and that the *how* is the domain of the creative process. In the intuitive process, the *hows* come in their own time and are really unimportant. All that is required is action on our part. When the intuitive door is opened, walk through it. Further intuitive insights will come, as required, to take us where we need to go.

All that is required is a simple releasing to the intuitive insight and the *will* to push forward and act. I say "simple," but we all know that the egocentric conditioning we have all undergone is difficult to overcome. For most of us, the egocentric chatter has been going on for a long time, and it will not relinquish control all that easily. The ego can be silenced, however, and needs to be if we are ever to realize our potential and if we are ever to be tuned in to the intuitive voice we all possess. We cannot have the awareness of gods through the filter of ego. The two are diametrically opposed to each other. Ego requires reason where intuition requires trust. We must abandon the voice of reason when the voice of intuition speaks. We must let go of our judgmental, egotistical tendencies that provide us with security in their controlling nature, and just let ourselves be guided by intuition. It is an abstract idea because we have fallen so far from comprehending our own intuitive natures. We are conditioned to see things through and anticipate every step of the way whereas intuition requires a free fall of acceptance only.

It is a little like the story of the young man who comes upon an old abandoned cabin in the woods and as he is about to step through the door to enter, he hears the intuitive voice clearly tell him not to go in. He does not go in; however, we are left wondering why. If we were there listening to the young man tell the story, we might ask: "What was in there? "Why did you not go in?" Even knowing he did not go into the abandoned cabin, we still want to know what possible reason he had for not going in. His only response can be, "I don't know…..I didn't go in!" Our egocentric need to know why just cannot accept that answer but that is the nature of intuition. We sense and we act—nothing more. To trust that intuition is working and everything will *be* as it should is anathema to the ego. Can you not feel the pull of ego and curiosity right now as you contemplate what was in the cabin that may have caused him to first, hear the intuitive voice and second, not go in? That is the nature of our conditioning and it should be the reverse. Intuition is the only voice we should hear and respond to but it isn't because we have been conditioned, by ego, not to trust it.

Ultimate awareness is the awareness of gods. It is the all-seeing eye from which nothing escapes and all things are perceived. We all have the awareness. It is going on every minute of our lives. We just don't see it and therein lies the challenge for us. In order to be *tuned in*, we must silence the chatter of mind and become acutely aware of our bodies and tune ourselves to the inner knowing that goes on constantly. It is always there. We just don't sense it through the noise of mind.

When the man and the woman partook of the fruit, their eyes were opened and they took on a new awareness that released them to every possibility in an infinite existence. They literally became as the gods to know infinite possibilities and in no way were they confined to the view of just what we see through the physical senses. Their eyes were fully opened and no limitation was placed on them. Limitation of awareness is the work of the serpent spoken of earlier. It is the ego trying to identify itself in the world of physical sensing. It is the endless struggle to relive the past and make it a constant part of the present moment where we lose our true power and perception of the wondrous spectacle going on around us. We have the instrument to perceive far and away beyond the limited world we see. In fact, we are the instrument! Every cell in our bodies is attuned to the infinite and our intuitive natures can hear the song of the infinite if we will listen. Awareness is like the "dews from heavens" and it settles upon us in the quietness of mind and the stillness of thought. *We are the awareness we seek!*

Chapter 10

Neutral Nature of God

In the context of the Genesis metaphor we have used before, it is often assumed that upon God's discovery that Adam and Eve had partaken of the fruit that they were cursed and punished for their willful disobedience. They were not. How could they be? God proclaimed the man and the woman to be as He was. Literally, Adam and Eve were gods as "They have become as one of us" knowing good and evil. A garden was no longer necessary or possible because Adam and Eve were going to begin their own creation. The garden was someone else's creation and while wonderful and plentiful as it was, it was not their creation and, as gods they would begin to experience their own creative processes.

Conscious awareness is all God supposedly "cursed" them with if we are to consider that a curse. "Instead of tilling my garden and eating from it, till your own." Create your own now that you are "one of us." Whether metaphorical or real, the message is the same to all of us. "Ye are gods" and gods taste the fruit of their own creating. Eve would now *feel* the physical pain of bearing children. Adam would *know* the exertion of creating his own posterity, abundance, and life—his reality, as it were. This is the gift of God – *knowing!* Not in the sense of a warehouse or an inventory of knowledge, but an awareness of everything happening within a new perception. His awareness was opened to a whole new manner of perception, that of gods. There is an ability to know or an acuity of knowing, or more precisely, a possibility of knowing all that *can* be known. In other words, you get to know now what gods know and in that knowing, you create the world you live in. "What ye sow, so shall ye reap."

Being like "us" now makes you responsible for everything you choose to create in your life. Pain, sorrow, happiness, joy—it matters not. It will take the same amount of creative energy to have pain and sorrow as happiness or joy. Prior to this new awareness, "I" gave you everything. Now that you are aware as "we" are aware, you must create your own worlds, and you will reckon with your own creating.

Your eyes have been opened to an infinite spectrum of possibilities and whatever you choose in that spectrum of possibilities is all and only for you to decide, create, and be responsible for. That is the freedom I give you. *That is freedom.* "In the sweat of thy face shalt thou eat bread" is really nothing more than saying "By your own creating, shalt you eat bread." Your awareness now allows you to fashion your life. Have the life you want. Construct it. When looked at in this light and considering all the possibilities available to us now, the Garden of Eden was a prison. Sure, everything we needed to survive was provided for, even abundantly so, but we didn't know it. No possibility, other than surviving, existed for us in the *unaware* state we were in while in the garden. Nothing else really mattered. Everything was made available to us.

Becoming gods and opening our awareness puts us in the unique position of having to take responsibility for our own acts of creation. This is what gods do. They create for themselves and have at their disposal all the inventive and constructive powers of the universe. The blueprint for invention also exists in the first few chapters of Genesis. And God said, "Let there be light and there was light." Gods *state* what they want and they get it. They don't list what they *don't* want, only what they do want. They command it, and it is so. And they look at what they create and call it good. Therefore, all creation is good. In other words, no creation is bad. This seems to nullify the concept of good and evil; the range of good and evil is a spectrum of possibility and nothing else. Good and evil are nebulous on a scale of infinity. Neither good nor evil exists at all, since all is created by gods. Gods don't create good or evil. They just create and it is all good. It can also be said that all creation is generic. It is neither good nor bad; it just *is*. In so describing that all creations are generic with no good or bad, then God is neutral and we should be so too.

God is neutral. That is to say that the creative power of the universe is unbiased. For God to be anything other than neutral would be to deny the infinite variety of every living or non-living thing on this planet or in the universe for that matter. How else could you possibly explain the various life forms as we know them and, perhaps more importantly, the different characteristics of the human family? Black, white, brown, short, tall, male, female, gay, straight, healthy, sick, weak, strong, brown-eyed, blue-eyed, curly-haired, straight-haired, big-footed, small-footed, it goes on and on and on. Only a neutral God could generate the diversity we have on the earth and call it *all good*. Only such a neutral God could promote free agency resulting in an earth that could exist as it does today. If God is neutral, then good and evil, which is a description of an infinite range of possibility, are neutralized because there is only good. Free agency demands a neutral God. *Creative power is neutral power*.

God would have to be unbiased in order to have created a world with all the variation that exists within it. If there really was only *one* right way, everything that is outside of that *right way* would be an easy thing to fix for a "one God creates all." Simply take away all possibilities that fall outside that *one right way*. Think about it. Removing all possibility for doing anything outside the *one right way* would put us back into the Garden of Eden. That's right! No possibility to do anything but the *one right thing* is a conditioned state not unlike that of Adam and Eve in the garden. The only possible exception they were given was that of an infinite and incredible variety of choices, all of which would come at their own beckoning, their own choosing, and as a result of their choosing, so it is done.

Who wouldn't choose the latter if given the choice to Adam and Eve in the garden? Live here and be provided for like all the other creatures on earth or *create your own earth in any way you choose it to be*. Be like the creatures of the earth or be like us? What would you choose if that was how it was presented to you?

The story of the creation of man and the Garden of Eden is the story of man becoming God, awakening to something profound and wondrous beyond anything that can be described in three-dimensional terms. Man bursts forth with all the creative power we attribute to a god who exists outside of ourselves, and whom we have created in *our* image, but have made him untouchable unlike ourselves. He can never be wrong, but we can. We can never be right, but he can. He is everything we cannot give to ourselves even though we are greater than anything we can conceive of as God-like and beyond any human capability. And to convince ourselves that we are less than God, we have created an elaborate scale of right and wrong to judge ourselves against so we are sure never to consider that "we are gods." How could we possibly be gods or even think to be as God when we have failed to measure up to all of the rules and qualifications *we have made* to judge ourselves against?

God never made any rules for Adam when He cast him out of the garden! Adam and Eve never received a memo from God outlining any policies they would have to abide by in order to be *saved*, nor were they given any criteria describing what constituted good or evil or right or wrong or what they could or couldn't do! Why? Doesn't it seem callous and mean to send Adam and Eve out on their own with no rules of engagement and no criteria for how they could once again have the kind of access to God they once had in the garden?

Consider that they wouldn't need it. Why would they? They were gods. Adam and Eve were not cast out of a life of good and plenty. They were cast *into* it! And as gods themselves, they could create any existence they wanted and not be held accountable in any way because it was neither *good nor evil*. They were given the ability to *know* good and evil, *not be judged by it!* God did not pass judgment on Adam and Eve when they partook of the fruit. He simply shared the consequence of their action which was to become as Himself, as God. Yes, he said, they would surely die, but they would have died anyway. The only difference now was that they would *live knowing* or being aware they would die. That's all. Dying was nothing more than becoming aware of it as an inherent or inevitable part of the human condition as well as all other animate forms in this life. It was the same for Eve in bearing children. Instead of bearing children as the animals do, she would have the *awareness* of the creation of life within her and she would *know* the bodily strain at childbirth, and through such knowing could identify it as both painful and joyous. The man and the woman would now feel, at a godlike level, the inner joy at creating life in every way. They would sense the emotion of every aspect of their newfound awareness, the awareness of gods! In other words, the man and the woman would feel sensation like pain, sorrow, joy, or happiness.

Feeling as a way of *knowing* is just one of the gifts of gods. Coming to a *knowing* of good and evil is nothing more than a description of how vast, even infinite, the range of knowing is. There is no good or evil! There is no right or wrong! Good and evil have been taken from their intended description of *infinite knowing* to a *scale* of finite reasoning that only perceives what is accepted in this reality. Our finite reasoning has attempted to surround the infinity we all exist in. It is crippling. We have systematically surrounded the unknown or unknowable with parameters we think they must conform to in order to become knowable. What we consider to be known has been classified with whatever our own particular *scale* of right or wrong dictates. There is no scale! Gods do not need one. Gods create out of infinite possibilities and it is all good! In other words, all creation is neutral. It is neither good nor evil, right nor wrong. Imposing a scale, rather than accepting good and evil as a neutral description, creates the basis for judgment which ultimately keeps us from knowing the vastness of creative power we possess. Everything that happens, every event no matter how great or small, simply is what it is without any applied scale or judgment.

It is only in neutrality that God can co-exist with so many other gods. Each of us, as gods, can create the world in whatever form we choose and since there is no right or wrong or good and evil, our world must exist in harmony with all other godlike creations. The only way this is possible is if we become unbiased ourselves and accept the creative abilities of everyone in existence on this and all other earths. In fact, the neutrality of God insists that being God is a very individual thing which we all tend to take for granted.

We often speak of those free-spirited individuals who run just outside of our constructed norms and we question their ability to ever be able to conform when, in fact, our own souls cry out to be exactly like that. Jesus' insistence that "I am the way, the truth, and the life" was the sublime recognition that he, as an individual, was the ultimate truth and consequently, the only way to life. It was a deeply individualistic remark to make but was said with great humility. Translated it might imply, "I am my own way, and truth, and life." He was not saying that somehow through him or because of him that *we are*. It was the supreme statement of who *he was*. He, like few others, understood his *oneness* with life and everything in existence – the ultimate "*I am*"-ness. He knew it and wanted all to know that within themselves, they had it too. He even predicted that in having done the miraculous things he did, that we could do, even *would* do, greater things. If his power to perform miracles was and continues to be considered God-like than his own prediction confirms the god-like nature of every one of us. "Greater things have I done will you do." Jesus saw the innate godliness in all mankind and implored us to accept it, but if we were to have difficulty seeing it in ourselves, then we should accept it because of him "in his name." "Believe that I am in the Father and the Father is in me. Or else believe me for the very works' sake. I will do what you ask of me, but you can do it of yourself without me."

"As I and my Father are one, so too will we enjoin you to us." We are all *one* connected physically and spiritually. There is none greater or lesser. We are all one and this is the message I bear to all. It is the ultimate message to all of life. We all exist on *par* with everything else and from this force all things are created by the power of thought. Thought permeates all things and all space and time, and the release of ourselves to it is the power by which we create our world, our universe, our reality, and the same power we have given to the god we have created in our image is power *we* possess! In some sense, it is even a greater power because our limited thinking has created a God that is limited by that thinking.

Being neutral permits us to accept everything we see in our existence and withhold any judgment of any kind. It simply allows for everything to be as it is. It is the ultimate state of seeing beyond any illusions of life to something far greater than anything we can imagine. The world is wondrous and beautiful beyond all the descriptions we ascribe to it but to see it without those descriptions is the only way we can know it as gods. Being in a neutral state is the only way to know our inner selves and it gives us eyes that perceive everything as wondrous and good.

Chapter 11

Fear of Being

Recall the parable of the talents spoken of in the New Testament where Jesus tells of a man traveling to a far country who leaves his wealth with his servants to manage until he returns. To one he gives five talents, to another he gives two, and to yet another he gives one. Upon his return from his travels he calls his servants to him to ask for an accounting of that which he had entrusted them with. The servant to whom he gave five talents was able to trade and increase it to ten talents and likewise the servant to whom he gave two was able to increase it another two to four. However, the servant to whom he gave one talent buried it and returned it to the master without any increase. In his explanation to the master, the servant identifies all the things his master was as far as the servant, and perhaps society, viewed him. He portrayed him as a "hard man," "reaping where he had not sown and gathering where he had not strawed." Finally, he explains that he was afraid of the master and thus hid the talent so he would be able to return it to the master without any reprisals should he have squandered it.

It is interesting how the master reacts to the servants in this parable. To the first two, he expresses pleasure and tells them they are good and wise. Yet with the third, he is angry and accusatory. He refers to him as 'wicked' and 'slothful' and further reprimands him for not banking the talent to make some interest on it. The master then responds in a surprising manner considering that the servant did not lose anything and was able to return the talent to his master. The master first takes the talent from him and gives it to the servant who had five to begin with and exclaims that "everyone that hath shall be given, but from him that hath not shall be taken away even that which he hath."

It is almost inconsistent with the other teachings of Jesus that the master should react this way to his servant who, after all, had not lost anything. Are we to understand from this that you are punished for not making money when you are given guardianship of someone else's money? Doesn't it sound somewhat cruel and inappropriate to be so hard on someone who, out of his own fear of loss, hid the talent so it could be returned to his master? Doesn't the master's response suggest "You're already lowly, so here's more lowliness"? It would seem on the surface that the "haves" gain more and the "have nots" have all they do have taken from them. Harsh indeed, but is this really what is meant?

This is not what Jesus was implying through this parable. He was speaking of opening yourself to something greater than what *you* are presently. In other words, increase your awareness of the world around you. *"Fear not what you are not!* I will not condemn you. You can only condemn yourself."

"For the Son of Man is come to seek and to save that which was lost." What was lost that Jesus speaks of? It was not our souls that were missing but *our own divinity!* Our sense of divine *I Am-ness* has been buried beneath a new sense of fear and loss, and has been overshadowed by the idea that we are sinful by nature and need to fear a vengeful God who will punish us. Somewhere along the so called "course of human development," we lost the knowing that *we* are the divine and that, just as in Eden, we walked and talked with God, "in the cool of the day," anytime we wanted. We lost our identity with our true selves to the noise of ego and the illusion of modern life. We have misplaced that knowing and Jesus sought only to show us, once again, how vast, wonderful, and divine we are! Our fears are so imposing that we have turned our focus to the outside world for solutions to all the trials we face in life. We have given way to the idea that we are the creators of our own universe and look elsewhere for guidance and direction that can only come from within. Our fears have become daunting and debilitating in the face of the awareness that we are so much greater than anything we can conceive of. For some of us, we do not fear what we are not, but instead what we are. In other words, we fear our greatness and accept the reality of this illusion because to admit to such greatness we believe carries a burden and responsibility to *real* life we choose not to embrace. It is easier to "follow the crowd."

Jesus often taught by means of parable or coded story that, while imparting something easily construed or applicable to the times, had underlying meaning that very few would grasp. Even after two thousand years, such meanings are still not understood, even though there are many interpretations. Most interpretations befit the ego since the ego seeks meaning in terms that satisfy its level of reason, understood in five-sense terms. Jesus knew that most would hear his parables and immediately apply rational reasoning, inferring meaning from the actual story rather than hearing his true meaning. He spoke in code, and in so doing, he revealed the secrets of the universe as well as clarified our divine nature. It was revealed, however, in such a way that if the ego was the overriding force in our lives, the true meaning would escape us. Even today, most hear the parables and take them literally which is exactly what was done when Jesus spoke them. It is easy to apply meaning to the story as it is read and assume we are among the few who actually grasp it.

We might easily interpret the parable of the talents to mean that we are to be wise stewards and that we should make good use of those things we are given. That is the obvious interpretation of the story's key elements. However, if the purpose of a parable is to hide deeper, less comprehensible meaning within it, then surely the obvious meaning cannot be what Jesus was referring to. When we consider the servant who protected the talent and was able to return it to the master, what was it specifically that he did wrong? He didn't lose his master's money. How did he err in presenting his master with the talent he was charged to be steward over? The obvious conventional wisdom tells us that we should not waste opportunities to better ourselves or what we have been given in this life. If we were to add to the story that the servant invested the money, but the investments were poor and he ended up losing the talent altogether, what might the master have done in such a case? While it is impossible to say, the obvious meaning is not the message we are supposed to internalize. What else is there?

Perhaps if we look at what the other two did or didn't do, we might find new meaning. When the first two were asked to give an accounting, they matter of factly stated that the five talents had grown into ten and the two into four. There was no talk of concern or any *how* given. They simply acted and stated the facts. The third servant, however, pointed out his great fear of the master and in having such fear, he was paralyzed from doing anything other than hiding the talent. In other words, his *fear* of the master prevented him from venturing out in anyway, even just putting the money in the bank and collecting interest. While *fear* as used in the context of the story does little more than add descriptive qualities to it, *fear and its opposite are the lesson!*

Jesus was reiterating, as he had often in the Gospels, that what you possess within is what is drawn to you. In other words, if you have fear, then the things of which you are afraid are what will be drawn to you in your life. It is the law of attraction or *like attracting like*. Those who *have* will have more and more because that is the nature of their attraction. Those who are in the mindset of "not having," will lose what they have because that is what they are attracting. They are attracting *not having* and the outcome of that attracting is to *not have*. You cannot bring into your experience that which you are afraid of receiving or that which you believe you are unworthy of. It is not enough to think about what you want and have it manifest itself in your reality. You must be in a state of being. What you are is the message conveyed to the universe. *Being* activates the thoughts that create our reality. As in the parable, the servant could not attract more into his reality because of his own fear of losing what he already had. His fear of loss was the nature of his being and that is what he brought into his experience which resulted in the master taking from him and giving to another. The symbolism of the story is that we are our own masters. In our reality there is no "master" standing over us taking away and giving as he pleases. We are the master spoken of in the parable and it is ourselves who make our experience what it is. Our state of being is our master and it is ourselves that "giveth and taketh away." We create everything in our reality and if having less is your mindset, then the outcome of that mindset is *less*.

You cannot stand in a place of fear and not be afraid!

Fear is something we bring to the table ourselves as is everything else in our experience and "as we bring it, so it is served unto us." The first two servants were seemingly unafraid of any consequences to be suffered at the hands of the master, and the effort they expended to create more wealth was no greater than the third servant's fear, resulting in doing nothing more than hiding the money. His fear prevented him from taking any action and it caused more things for him to be afraid of. His state of having was in fact a condition of fear, and in that state he invited the circumstances of fear to appear in his experience.

Fear cripples us because *we* let it. It is of our own making and regardless of what we fear, we will draw it to us like a magnet and we will not escape it until we come to realize that we have control over it. We end fear by embracing it! The paralyzing effect of fear that keeps us from moving forward is like a huge door calling attention to the very things that limit our freedom. Embracing fear is pushing the door open. Recognizing fear is nothing more than becoming aware of the barrier we construct around ourselves that not only locks our divine nature deep within, but also prevents it from ever getting out!

We often speak of "the fear of failure" but in reality there is no such thing as failure in an infinite universe! Fear of failing is derived from the original notion of good and evil and this line of thinking has the effect of putting us into situations of our own making where we will be judged by a favorable or unfavorable set of criteria. We let ourselves get so caught up in the illusion that everything we do is being scrutinized by some unseen force that actually cares one way or the other what the outcome will be. We plant that seed in our own minds and let it control our existence! Nothing the master did had anything to do with the servant acting as he did. The servant, of his own accord, allowed what was said or known about the master to take root in his own mind and with such thinking could not act out of anything but fear that he would be judged in a certain way if he lost the talent. The master didn't do that to him! He did it to himself! His fear of a preconceived judgment paralyzed him and that fear is what he realized anyway! What is the message we need to get from this parable?

This is it: "That which you are is that which you have." If you are fearful, you will have fear. If you are sad, you will have sadness. If you are joyful, you will have joy. If you are happy, you will have happiness. In fact, you cannot realize your own divinity, your own godlike nature unless *you know that you have it!* That is the ultimate message of the parable. *Fear not what you think you are not!* Be what you are and you are gods! We are filled to overflowing with divinity and power, not from on high but from within. It is always there but our fear, like a door locked shut, keeps us from ever seeing it. What you do not have, you cannot get unless you literally enter a state of having. That which you have can never be taken from you, and the most important recognition of *having* we must all come to is that we are divine! *We are the god we fear!* The master never took anything from the servant. The servant never had anything to give. That is the point we must get from this story. We are all gods until we choose to give it away through fear, or sadness, or anger or whatever other emotion we allow to control us in any given situation. Be that which you are by *being that which you are!!* What you are can never be taken from you. It can only be given away − by you. There is no unseen force taking from those who have not and giving it to those who have. We are in absolute control.

Reviewing the story we can ask, "Of the three servants who had the biggest ego?" Whose ego had the greatest control over its host? While we can't know from the story what the motivations of the other two servants were, it is clear that the ego of the third servant was very concerned that the master was powerful and took what he wanted and that he could suffer greatly at the hands of the master. His ego was debilitating enough to convince the man that the option of doing nothing was the best of other choices before him. To carry this, further why would the master come down so hard on the servant for his lack of action? It is likely to *crush* the ego of that servant. Remember that to the man and the woman was given power to crush the head of the serpent? Regardless of the emotion on display, whether it be fear, sadness, anger, etc., we must crush it so it cannot have a crippling affect upon us. *Ego will always deceive!*

Law of attraction gives according to that which we have. It is the great law of creation. Our state of being manifests itself in our state of having, or vice versa. We can change our state of *having* simply by changing our state of *being*, for instance be afraid, have fear, etc. Being leads to having. Having reinforces being.

Otherwise the story leads us to conclude that the *haves* get more and the *have nots* get less and less. The lesson is to fear not that which you do not have and perhaps even more so, to not fear anything we perceive to be standing in the way of that having. Fear of any kind keeps us stuck or glued to what we are and all of our past outcomes. Fear locks all doors that if opened would set us free.

Fear is really nothing more than conditioning. It is something once attempted that didn't work out as planned or the systematic persistence by parents, teachers, friends, etc., that we need to be fearful of things that their own conditioning led them to. Such conditioning, over time, becomes a story that begins, "This is *how* I became afraid." It actually becomes a part of the story of us that ego puts on display as a virtue rather than being another device that hinders us from knowing who we really are. Fear cannot exist in a mind that knows no *how*. Isn't that the point? If you break down what is feared, it always breaks down into *not knowing* an outcome or having experienced an undesirable outcome and fearing its happening again. It is always associated with a past experience that ended up differently than we had expected or planned for or that we have become convinced of through conditioning. In either case, we are paralyzed by the effects and fear becomes just one of the many crippling emotions we accept as a part of our nature.

Through *expectation* and planning, fear finds its way into our egocentric score card. Expectation and planning is the *how* the ego always seeks when creative thoughts or intuitive knowledge enters our minds. Ego struggles for certainty in all things even though nothing is certain. Outcomes manifest themselves in their own way and time. The *how* will be known but only after it is revealed from the unknown. This contrast is what causes fear. Not knowing *how* causes the ego to fill itself with expectation and planning or to do nothing. The outcome usually leads to more fear because reality is so different from all the planning and expectation. Fear is the difference between what ego insists is knowing and the unknown. Ego is what becomes afraid. Inner self or the god we are is all accepting of every outcome regardless of any notion of a *preplanned outcome.*

An interesting phenomenon of fear is that it is always associated with an unknown. We even categorize 'fear of the unknown' as a classification of many labeled fears, yet the projection of past events, traumas, and taboos into a current or future event is the basis for fears. Since nothing can be done to alter the past or insure the future, the future and past are unknowns that have no bearing whatsoever on anything occurring in the present. In other words, all fear is derived from the unknown. Past experience or future anticipated experience has no affect on anything in the present unless *we* allow it to.

In the course of human life, there are no knowns other than that which we are experiencing in this very moment. Accordingly, we should fear everything in our experience simply because we can never know the outcome of any action, yet we don't. Why not?

Fears come in two forms and are manifested as worry which is very stressful to both body and soul. The first way fears come about is from the trauma-based projection of a past event into the present moment. It is part of the junk we store in our historical data banks that paralyzes us from taking action but also drains us of the energy we need to walk through life. Consider that a past event that may have taken minutes or hours to occur commands the rest of your life from that point on. Such a past event has power over our volition and will, for no other reason than we allow it to.

The fear itself has no power nor does the act or event that caused the fear to begin with. It only has power because we allow the chatter of mind, the ego, to convince us that the event has a long term impact on us and always will. As rational as ego tries to be, it never is. It can't be because fear is always irrational and based in finite terms. Fear caused from past events drags with it all the anxiety and stress originally felt through our life to the present. It is like an anchor that puts continuous drag on our life physically, emotionally, and spiritually and all for mere moments in *past time*. What a loss!! We literally give ourselves, our power, to fear!

The other form of fear is that of unknown outcomes we project into the future. It is worry and stress over events we can't possibly have any control over so we worry about possible negative outcomes with the hope they will not come to pass. Sometimes we worry to the point of obsession which almost always paralyzes us from taking any action. Fear is always based in some negative outcome and worry is always a by-product of fears, be they based in the past or future. Fears, derived from past events or from unrealized future events both have form in the unknown.

Fears are just a part of the egocentric tool kit developed to keep the divine self so afraid of itself that life is lived in an illusory, if not, altered state. Ego is a master at using the tools of its tool kit to manipulate any situation to its own ends. Fear is the trauma-based projection of the past into the present or the worry of some unknown *how* that may or may not happen in the future. It is part of the junk we store in our historical data banks. Fear is a crippler, an energy drain and a major cause of our disconnection from our godlike nature.

The paradox is that fear is born of the unknown and to live a completely intuitive life, we must fully accept the unknown because it surrounds every aspect of our lives. Fear is born of the unknown in the sense that any past or future event cannot have power unless we sanction it and while the past is believed to have been our own experience, remember that life is an illusion. What we experience in this three-dimensional experience is what we have been conditioned to perceive and it is so minute when compared to the reality that is there, throughout. What we think of as our past experience is really the recollection of the illusion we were living at that time and it can only have power in our present lives if we bring it into the present. We don't have to do that. Likewise the fear of the future is an unknown. We can give the power of the present moment to a future expectation but it is always of our own choosing and always a waste of our power because we cannot know what lies ahead. Whatever our expectation of the future is, we fret over something that does not exist in any reality. The future is a complete unknown to anyone.

Our power as gods comes in present time. There is no past or future in an infinite universe. Such power can only exist in our minds if we provide the reasons for them and all our fears would be washed clean if we could comprehend the infinite nature of ourselves. Fear is an egotistical device that traps us in our own history (past) or the unnecessary expectation of some future event that does not exist. Do not fear. Move throughout life with knowing, a knowing that can only come in present time and in that knowing fear is no more.

Chapter 12

Humility – The Unimportance of Self

Humility is the ultimate act of acceptance. It is an acceptance that everyone, indeed everything, in our perceptive world is equal to everything or everyone else. Humility is a condition where no judgment exists and the idea or concept of right and wrong or good and evil has no place in our thinking. It is the ultimate letting go of all that we think is important and the fundamental acceptance of our divine nature. Our only intent is to connect to that inner knowing we all have, but in doing so, we remain neutral about the acts of others who are not doing the same.

Humility requires us to shed all judgments or our reasoning that categorizes any act as right or wrong. It requires we release those constructs that we use to rate our importance with that of others. Humility requires no duality of any kind and indeed seeks it not. It only sees a spectrum of events that all fall within the range of possibilities, and of which we are all capable. Humility requires no acts or expectations of contriteness since it accepts all things just as they are; any act of contriteness is an act of self importance. The humble individual has no need for demonstration of any kind, large or small, for therein lies the idea that there is a judgment of some kind causing the very nature of things to lose their equality.

Humility requires shedding the weight of any form of self importance, including all roles and positions that establish guidelines for us. It is also crucial that we see others without those same guidelines. Humility simply *accepts!* It accepts that others are not humble and that some expect accolades and recognition even when they would say of themselves that they are humble. Humility needs no recognition but allows for those who do, for in reality they "know not what they do." There is no righteous indignation as there is no righteousness. There is simply "being" and in that "being," infinite splendor and wonder are a part of our innate nature. No thing is greater or less than anything else.

We sometimes think of those who are humble as those who are without basic physical comforts such as food, clothing, or shelter. When we define "poor people," we often say they are "of humble circumstances." Many of our great spiritual leaders are often thought to be humble because they have shed all of their worldly possessions and have taken vows of poverty. Poverty is somehow equated with humility, but as long as there is an idea that humility has a description of any kind, it is no longer humility. There is no concept of humility. As soon as there is, it is no longer humility. Humility carries no weight and no burdens of any kind, including poverty. It is attached to no form of self importance whether that form of self importance states, "I must be rich" or "I must be poor." Either side of the coin is a degree of self importance.

Some definitions of humility speak of a "lowly opinion" of oneself, but that is wrong. Humility is having "no" opinion of yourself, none whatsoever. *The absence of a definition of oneself is humility.* That is the neutral, all-accepting position of a truly humble person. Any opinion that we carry of ourselves or of others removes any description of humility from us whether it is a lowly or haughty one. Humility simply has no opinion and exists in the sweetness of life that lives abundantly and fully without judgments of any kind or any expectation that lies outside the true inner self. The humble individual takes in life fully and profusely, and accepts all things as part of a grand spectacle we are all a part of. The humble individual understands that in the realm of infinity, nothing is greater than anything else. Everything is wondrous!!

When Jesus was referred to by a disciple as 'good,' he pushed back with "Why callest thou me good? There is none good but my Father." In other words, there is "no" good, just as there is no bad—no judgment whatsoever. No description, no verbalization, no thinking. Simply being is humility. That is where God is and it is the only place we can know "Him as ourselves."

"Blessed are the *poor* in spirit, for they shall inherit the kingdom of God." What is a "poor" spirit? Is it someone who is destitute, hungry, or without education or lowly social status? Is it someone who is without creature comforts as we have come to call them? Is it someone who has been knocked down by the so-called travails of life? Is it someone whom we deem humble? None of these are what makes us "poor" in spirit because they all require some form of identity that carries weight, or the baggage we include with these forms or definitions. For the person with the identity, it is "poor me" while for the observer, it is "poor you." *You are not humble when in the prescribed position nor are you humble when you are feeling sorry for the one who is.*

"Poor in spirit" is a spirit without any definition. In literal terms, it is a spirit that carries no baggage of any kind. It is a spirit that is "poor" or without all the things we load ourselves up with throughout our lives regardless of whether they are judged good or bad. Baggage is baggage. Excessive weight is heavy regardless of whether it consists of good intentions or bad, and our conditioning has lead us all to believe that there is something uniquely important about us that makes us who we are. Despite this fact, none of it is unique or important in an infinite reality that sees everything in existence as incredible! To be poor in spirit is to be free of the idea of any importance we or anyone else must define and measure up to. A humble individual is poor in spirit and within them *is* "the kingdom of heaven." They are light and fluid and without the heaviness the *rich* in spirit have.

Jesus used the metaphor that it would be "more difficult for a rich man to get into heaven then for a camel to go through the eye of a needle." We've all heard the story. He wasn't talking about just monetary riches. Riches come in many forms. It is possible to be "rich" in poverty. To be rich in poverty is to be loaded up with all the identity that goes with your description of poverty. People wear these circumstances like a badge of honor and are almost proud to show it off to others so as to secure some sort of honor for being in that condition. We can be rich in sickness. How many times do we see people identify themselves "as their illness"? We've seen people introduce their disease before giving their name and then sharing their story elaborately and painstakingly so others can pay tribute to their suffering with pity or sympathy. Those are the riches they seek. Pity, sympathy, and other forms of recognition or riches of the spirit as it were. Recognition for their pain and suffering and the drama of their particular life is playing out. Those are the riches Jesus is talking about.

The opposite of a poor spirit is a rich spirit. Rich in what? Rich in the junk of life: the history, the drama, the identity with whatever objects or thoughts we can gather to us. Why did Jesus target the rich or materially wealthy man to teach us this lesson? Because we can all relate to "things" or having the monetary wealth as something we have all wanted, have, or have had and want again. We all know what that feels like, but Jesus's point was not that the man had wealth and riches, but rather that we must cease to "want" altogether. We must let our spirits be poor, not rich. We must not "want" in the way the world wants because that wanting enriches our spirit with the very things that keep us from finding heaven within.

Having riches and wanting more is no more than being sick and wanting attention or being poor and wanting pity. Most of us don't even know we solicit abundance or riches, if you will, that supports and surrounds our story, our identity. Consider how hard it really would be for someone of great wealth to sell all that they had and follow Jesus. And for what purpose? Into a ministry? No, follow Jesus into a life of identity with oneself, more specifically, the inner self or the God within that he spoke of constantly. Follow Him into that path, the path of true discovery. He was not telling us to follow a religious or philosophical path, rather he wanted us to journey like him into a true state of being-ness. Follow with me into a state of awareness the likes of which nothing you now know compares to. Even at that, it is a difficult thing to do, for a man of wealth and means. Why a rich man of means and not a poor man of means? During Jesus' three years, we call his ministry, there wasn't an abundance of poor people selling what they had and following him. What was Jesus talking about?

Monetary wealth and abundance or the "rich man" is a metaphor for non-material wealth, the stuff of the mind. Junk collected and stored in the cellar of the mind, while rarely used, is heavily guarded, added to, and hoarded. Letting go of those things, "selling" as it were, is far more difficult than physical things. Material things and wealth, etc., can be taken from us at anytime, and while to lose those would be painful and difficult, our thoughts, our inventory of ideas, beliefs, identifying histories, and stories cannot. They are locked away in our minds in the safety of vaults no bank depository compares to.

However, to know that we are gods requires that we let go of all that inventory, and to become poor in spirit. These are all the riches stored away over a lifetime of learning *how* to view our descriptions of the world as we know it. This is what is required and Jesus has already told us how difficult it would be for a rich man to do it.

It is nearly impossible! Not because it cannot be done but because we put the chains of riches around us and cannot get past the idea that we have all the power to remove them! It is amazing what we do to ourselves over a lifetime of conditioning and adherence to a story that, having no real power, completely controls us. We hear it in conversations almost daily how people overcome one thing or another to get to where they are now. They might have overcome poverty or learning disabilities, or physical limitations of one kind or another, losses of loved ones, etc., all of which add to a rich and abundant story that we believe is what gives us identity. These are not our identity and carrying the weight of these so called "identifiers" is not the way to finding the truth of who we really are. We are gods and no good or bad remnant from our past will ever bring us to that realization! We must become poor in spirit to find the heaven within us. How rich and abundant is your story? What is your inventory of life identifiers? What is the junk in the closet of your mind?

"Poor in spirit" means to be free of riches of the spirit and without abundance without the weight of excess baggage we accumulate and carry with us throughout or lives. Riches and abundance of what? Only the things our thinking can attach to our spirit. This is the abundance of things we constantly review in our minds and tell ourselves about. It matters not *what* we are rich in. Jesus referred to the Sadducees and Pharisees, the religious and secular leaders of his time, as being openly pious so that all could recognize them for their goodness and worthiness. These were the riches they sought and it is no different from seeking material wealth and abundance. Piety might be the spiritual equivalent to riches or wealth. Being pious requires a huge energetic effort to maintain and Jesus specifically said not to be that way. Wealth comes in many forms other than material wealth and it is from this wealth that our reality fills up with more and more weight and responsibility.

Perhaps another way to look at it might be in terms of conspicuousness. There is nothing wrong with having wealth and riches just as there is nothing wrong with devotion to religious or spiritual things. What Jesus emphasized about devout religious leaders of the day was their conspicuousness, the showing of their piety and devotion. They wanted others to recognize their piety and confirm for them the identity they worked so hard to establish. That was a form of wealth to them and it was the riches of conspicuous piety they sought, just as with the man with great riches was challenged to give all away. Such an act would be difficult because of his identity with it. He was known to everyone and certainly to Jesus as a "rich man." It was through the conspicuousness of his wealth that he came to be known as such. The weight of material wealth is no different than that of piety or anger, or holding grudges, worry, fear, or all the other parts of ourselves that make up our identity. It would be just as difficult as it would be to give up material wealth so to is it difficult to give up the wealth of all the things we hold as part of the identity we project to the world.

A rich spirit is a heavy spirit just as a man rich in the things of this world is heavy and full of responsibility to keep, protect, and add to that wealth. A poor spirit has no need to keep, protect, and add to itself. It is light, fluid, and agile, free to move about at will and go where it wants unfettered by any weight or responsibility of any kind. It is impossible to hurt in a mental, emotional, or spiritual way the "poor" in spirit. They have no identity to which they can be tied and therefore no life arguments to defend or emotional weaknesses. The poor in spirit have no ego and therefore are not attached to the past conditionings that have occurred in their lives that make up identities as we know them. They have lost sensitivity to those things that the rest of us take offense at and allow to hurt us mentally, emotionally and spiritually. In truth no one has the power to hurt us mentally, emotionally or spiritually unless we ourselves identify with events, circumstances, or fears, and let that identity become so much a part of our reality that we feel a need to defend it. To those who are poor in spirit, humble as it were, all things are equal; therefore, nothing can harm the soul and make us hurt in the typical ways we are accustomed to. The poor in spirit have nothing to be hurt with or by!

Isn't it interesting that Jesus had no story. He lived by intent and by will. He never used himself, his childhood, or any part of his life as a point of reference the way almost all of us do today. He never referred to a "when" or a "where" concerning his life in his teachings to the masses. He made no reference to his childhood, or upbringing, or lessons learned along the way. We really know nothing about him from his own lips. We have some stories recounted about his birth and his visit to the temple when he was twelve, but beyond that, he is a complete mystery as a youth, adolescent, and young adult. Then out of seemingly nowhere, he burst onto the scene with a message so radical yet profound that it cannot be understood to this day. Who was Jesus? Why did he never divulge any story about himself that we can identify him with? Where was he in those years from age twelve to thirty? Why are we not given any credentials for his ministry, as it were, and where did this strange power with which he demonstrated miracles and his teachings come from? He completely confounded the wisest, most brilliant minds of the day and yet we know nothing of or about him. Anyone trying to pull off what he did today without education and sanctions of some kind would be institutionalized!

Even Jesus' life defied all precedence and he is accepted worldwide as a savior to people who know nothing more about him other than that he died on a cross, supposedly for our sins. What was it that gave him such great command of power? Recognizable power to even the greatest among the people of his day. Such questions have been asked then and continue to be asked now. They are questions that have legitimacy in the ego driven world we live in now, but they were of no importance to Jesus nor are they to anyone else who is "poor in spirit."

Those kinds of questions or credentials are asked by the ego satisfying, identity driven mind. By what authority "do you come?" The ego wants to know this. Even now great speculation centers around who he was, his circumstances, upbringing, education, etc., but all anyone can come up with is an idea based on conditions and customs of the time. People assume that he must have looked and dressed a certain way, and lived in poor working class conditions, that educational opportunities would have been minimal, etc. These are speculations based on what we understand about the times he lived in. There are, however, really no clues as to how he developed the clarity of mind and soul to know that he was god and had the power he taught us we all had as well. He was completely unconcerned about the so-called education and rules that constituted a righteous man and knew that he or any of us, in the lowest form, was greater than anything their education and rules could conceive of. We know nothing of where this came from!

No one can explain where his deeply seated ideas about humankind came from. The idea that heaven resides within every individual was so radical, yet we have no way of knowing where he developed such ideas. As far as the time and place he grew up in, outside of eastern philosophies, such ideas were not known or taught that we know of. We cannot point to a teacher or philosopher of his time or a place who was teaching such doctrine. It is an unexplainable mystery and nothing Jesus did in his three year ministry gives us a clue as to the seeds of his profound new ideas about God, man, and heaven.

But then again, why should he? His life was the very essence of how a life can be lived and how not hauling around the baggage of history and identity can free you to perform the miracles he did and even greater ones should you choose. The things we tie our identity to are the very things that attach us to the egocentric nature of our current reality, our illusions, if you will. They are the things that overshadow our godlike nature and prevent us from knowing the power Jesus demonstrated throughout his life. By his own words, we should be able to do everything he did and even more! Why don't we see more of this in a so-called "Christian world"? It is because we have been conditioned to accept another reality for ourselves that is not capable of such things. A reality that is egocentric in nature and which requires sensory proofs, credentials, and structural learning. We can change this but only when we let go of the idea that we are less than the gods, we in fact, are!

Giving up one's identity, or those things we identify with, is extremely difficult just as it is difficult to throw out the unused "things" we store in our cellars and basements. As regards to physical things we gather to us, we form sentimental attachments long after the useful life of such things are gone. Holding on to physical riches or mental riches is no different when it comes to the energy expended. They both require energy to hold and they are both difficult to let go of. For some it is impossible, or so it seems, when confronted with the prospect of letting go of the "story" associated with mental memory or physical *things*. Such memories often stir up all the emotion and intensity they originally had and while the story lay dormant for perhaps years or decades, its memory evokes tremendous emotion and energy utilization, energy that is not available to or for anything else.

Identity with things or mental constructs goes to the core of self-importance. It is as if to say that whatever the reasons for our emotional attachments to things or mental constructs are, they are more important than anything else in the world. Sometimes we defend "what is ours" to the death. Typically, the ego is about preservation of itself but occasionally it will hold a position so strongly, even unconsciously, that it can no longer yield to something other than that position. In such cases ego has lost all reason, even under threat or force, and will sacrifice itself for that position. Think about it. The ego would allow the body to die over a strongly held conviction or physical property. On a grander scale, wars are waged over the same things when the collective identity is challenged in such a way. How absurd!

The individual ego or collective ego would give up its own host to protect its identity even "knowing" that to do so will end itself all because the "all important" identity must be preserved at all costs.

You cannot know your inner self, your godlike nature when you believe that your feelings of sadness, or anger, or happiness, or unhappiness, or judgments of any kind are important. The greatest challenge we as humans have in this life is to overcome those feelings of self importance and to fight against the need for our ego to "be" important. Our acts, whatever they may be judged as, are unimportant. Whether viewed as greatly good or bad, they are unimportant. As soon as we let outside recognition for our acts, good or bad, be a measure of value or non-value of any kind or degree we have fed the ego, it's all important *self-importance*. Even "caring," as we all like to think we possess when applied conspicuously, is an act of self-importance.

The ego is a pig. It will gobble up anything put in front of it and it doesn't matter if it is perceived as something good or something bad. It will create a cover story regardless and spin whatever, however it best suits itself. We must shut that off or we will never know our true nature.

God needs a Garden of Eden to dwell in, not a place where the voice of the serpent, the endless chatter of mind, resides.

We cannot know God in the presence of the serpent. As the story goes, Adam and Eve roamed the Garden of Eden naked, without guilt of any kind prior to partaking of the fruit of the tree. Was partaking of the fruit somehow a reason that being naked was now something to be ashamed of? The serpent pointed out that they were naked but why was it suddenly a bad thing they needed to be ashamed of? It wasn't. As previously described, the serpent is a metaphor for the thinking man or egotistical mind. The determination that being naked was not appropriate or something to be ashamed of was the first judgment or rule to come forth out of Adam's and Eve's thinking minds. It is the first outcome of the ego attaching its identity to something it decided, or judged, was good or evil. This is the metaphorical beginning of an ego-centered identity. We're naked, not good—Better get dressed!

Knowing good and evil is not the cause of *being* good or evil. *Trying to decide what is good and what is evil "is"!* In other words, "identity" is directly linked to that which we judge either as good or evil. Judging, therefore, is a cause or creator of identity and until we stop the game of believing we know "what" is good and what is evil, we will never know God. We will never know who we are, or realize the full potential of "what" we are until we remove from ourselves the need to judge or hold duality of any kind and stop carrying around unimportant self identities that open us up to the so-called concerns of others. Humility knows no such differences or identities!

Judgment breeds identity and identity breeds self-importance. Self-importance blinds us to greater awareness. History is replete with stories in which an institutional identity condemned greater awareness and enlightenment. Consider Galileo Galilei who championed the Copernican idea that the planets revolved around the sun contrary to the popular religious dogma of the time that stated Earth was the center of the universe. The institutional identity at that time was so locked into its idea of reality that any form of scientific evidence to the contrary was grounds for a death sentence. Galileo was forced to recant his work about the universe and lived under house arrest the remainder of his life for having such ideas. Institutional self-importance silenced one of the greatest minds the world had ever known simply because it had determined that such an abstract idea was not known to them and therefore could not be!! Humility doesn't care!! Not to the individual or to the institution. With humility, all things are possible.

Again, Adam and Eve, as the story goes, lived in a state of innocence and endless goodness. They supposedly lived in a state completely devoid of good or evil. We might call it a natural, benign state. All of a sudden, in a symbolic act of disobedience, they become as the gods "knowing good and evil." What did this new awareness consist of? Was it really good and evil they came to know or was it the possibility of knowing all things? We cannot know for sure but *self importance* would assume that what we currently believe about anything is how Adam and Eve must have seen it, and that for anyone to see it differently makes them wrong or evil. Consider the presumption that your view of things could possibly apply to all people through all of history, presently and into the future. Most would agree that such an assumption would be the height of self importance. Yet it is not wrong to believe that your own individual perspective is always right, but we must always be aware that it is nothing more than that: *your individual view*. It is nothing more and its only application is to you. Where we err is only when we decide or judge that what we believe must apply to everyone else. That is self importance. In one context, it is tyranny and we would condemn tyranny in any form and stand against it. Yet to hold the view that what we believe as right or wrong is applicable to anyone else is tyranny. Tyranny, in its most blatant form, is the stripping away through force or coercion of anyone's right to think and act as *they* believe. In its subtlest form, it is what our mind judges to be best for someone else but is unable to enforce. It is a tyrannical mind that does either. In either case, it is the height of self importance to suppose that what we know to be good for ourselves must be equally good for everyone else.

Self importance is directly linked to the amount of emotional inventory we have in the closet of our mind. Some mental inventory is often linked to physical things stored in our attics and closets such as high school memorabilia, childhood toys or clothes, and any number of things we collect along the way. Nonetheless, there is emotional energy attached to those material things and it is the emotional energy that gets used up on "things" or "ideas" that cannot possibly lead to an awareness of self. Giving energy to such things can only lead us away from it. How often we look at items we have stored in our attics or basements and feel the rush of emotion connected with them. Even when we have the intention of throwing things out that we know we will never use, we can't let go. The emotional energy attached to these things is too great for us to give them up and so they go back into the spaces and clutter we intended to clean up. Memories are no different and when they are triggered, we glimpse first hand the emotion and energy needed to hold them in our minds. Again, such energy cannot be used for anything else. *We literally give our energy away to things that can no longer hurt us!!*

Somehow we all know this. We sometimes find ourselves in moments of frustration, doubt, sadness, concern, or self-reflection and ask, "Is this all there is?" We may even ask ourselves why we let such things bother us. Why do we indulge in things that are so old and petty? Sometimes this may lead us to explore more deeply to understand by asking questions such as "Who am I?" or others like it that seem to express a dissatisfaction with, perhaps, who we really are, or what we are all about.

Ego is quick to steer us away from this kind of inner dialogue because it knows that it cannot exist should the discovery of self be made and such an awareness can only be made in the depths of humility and quietness of mind. Ego also knows that its best defense is to stop such deeply seated thoughts and bury them in an ocean of noise and chatter, finally redirecting the soul within that ever searches, back toward the idea of self importance. It is difficult to break through that noise but the ego is quick to find a way, a circumstance that it can throw itself back into that will quiet such soulful thoughts. Ultimately we get back to looking at our inventory and the judgments it carries without ever having had a chance to answer those "other" questions.

In our ego driven world, we have even gone to great lengths to protect the ego from any onslaught of possible defamation or humiliation on a collective scale. A lot of our so-called political correctness is aimed at this. It is unthinkable to "hurt the feelings" of another, but it is only an egotistical identity that has been fueled and fed over a lifetime that can be hurt! Emotions are the ego's way of finding *place* in the world of other egos that are both susceptible to being hurt but also the cause of hurt. Our so-called feelings can be hurt. The humble cannot be hurt!! The humble are detached from their feelings because feelings are an egocentric device to keep us energetically attached to the events and circumstances of our past. It is a part of the conditioning we all experience from the moment we are born. Over and over again we are told that we should feel one way or another when we experience certain things and we carry those learned responses throughout our lives and into everything we do including relationships with others. Feelings that can be hurt are part of the noise and chattering that never ceases in our heads.

Our conditioning has taught us to make choices or judgments about everything going on in our world. It is almost a requirement of this reality to find a category or mood to put ourselves in based on the various situations we find ourselves in. "Am I happy or am I sad?" "Is it good or is it bad?" "Is it right or is it wrong?" Additionally, to succumb to any of our so-called emotional states to such a degree that they become conspicuous displays is to put one's self above that of others and it is an act of ego to draw attention to itself regardless of whether it is lowliness or haughtiness.

All of this questioning, judging, and displays of emotion are the box we put ourselves in and expect others to be in with us. Humility is a completely emotionless and neutral state and it accepts everything without judgment of any kind. Humility can only exist in a quiet mind that is unencumbered by any reasoning that justifies our particular existence or experiences above or below those of others. It simply accepts all before it without any *why* or *wherefore*, without need or benefit.

The humble person never asks about differences between things. Indeed such a person has no need to consider differences and therefore accepts "what is" as "what is." There is neither good nor bad, simply acceptance of whatever is happening in present time. The truly humble person stops time and exists in the purity and peace of now where the past is unimportant and the future is unknown. It is a purity of the essence of life that transcends all things, all emotion and moods. It is the place where our divine nature is no longer hidden in an illusion and we view all things in life with eyes that have no prejudice of any kind. It is the purest form of existence and the only way to access the god that each of is.

Humility is the nemesis of ego, or the antithesis. It is everything ego is not and ego cannot accept humility without losing itself. Identity and self importance are all the ego cares about and both require a "placement" or "alignment" of some kind which necessitates a duality that makes *choice* a major part of our existence.

Ego needs the recognition that it is acting a certain way no matter how subtly it manifests itself. Ego thrives on this and will find a way to achieve it regardless of whether it finds it in meager or abundant circumstances. On the other hand, with humility, there is nothing to gain just as there is nothing to lose. All things, events, and circumstances are equal and therefore need no judgments. Humility sees no duality and recognizes that in a reality of infinite possibilities there are no right or wrong choices. There is only action. Gods are humble and act out of *will*, not out of caring. They understand that caring is what connects them to the egocentric reality we live in. When living from *will*, their acts are deliberate and energetic and their power, as was Jesus', is recognizable beyond any conventional learning or credentials... To know the god you are, humble yourself, as did Jesus and all great spiritual teachers throughout history have and let go of any part of your identity that brings out any emotion. The things that upset us most and bring out strong reaction are likely the things we need to let go of. The energy they carry to exert strong reactions is energy that cannot be used to know God. In order to truly know God, know thyself. Ego self is unimportant. To know yourself is to know God.

Chapter 13

Energetic Being

Everything in the universe is energy including ourselves and has always existed in some form. The reasoning of man tends to always look for rationalizations or explanations for everything that goes on in our reality, and our reasoning becomes the basis for why we act, do, or say the things we do. The mind of man wants to know *why* or *how* for everything that goes on, and does so by attempting to put everything into quantifiable ideas and descriptions that please our reasoning but overlook any other possibilities. The very idea, and it is certainly not an idea, that we are energetic should open so many more possibilities to us to consider as *possible!* Every part of us vibrates and is a part of everything in the known and the unknown universe. Nothing that man can create with his intelligence and hands even begins to describe how great he is. We have risen to incredible heights and pushed ourselves to daring and fascinating depths of exploration, learning, and understanding about our existence and everything in it, but none of that begins to account for *what we are!*

As an energetic being, man, indeed all things, are mysterious in some way. Actually, they are, as are we, mysterious in numerous and incredible ways. Yet not being able to see beyond our own reason is what confines our perception to only those things we are conditioned to perceive and we miss the energy and vibration of all things. You might call it "universal life" but whatever it is called, it is infinite and endless and we are as much a part of it as it is a part of us. Just as energy is movement, so too is all of life. Everything we see and don't see moves. The movement many be faster or slower, but always into and out of form. It is always real, abundant, and never ending.

We have often heard the saying that "God moves in mysterious ways." Such a description of God allows him to remain a mystery while at the same time placing us in a light that can never achieve that same mysteriousness. It is interesting that we allow our gods to be mysterious and wondrous and do not give ourselves the same consideration. Man is mysterious and wondrous beyond anything we can comprehend in a rational or reasonable way, and yet our thinking continuously judges us as *what we are not* compared to a mysterious God we have created in that same mind. If man performs a miraculous or mysterious act, there must be a reason whereas if God does it, it remains mysterious. Even "miraculous."

The reasoning of man has rationalized us into something far less than we really are. The reasoning of man has failed to look at man as an energetic being that is without beginning or end, and is unlimited in his ability to create, just as the mysterious gods we have created are capable of. In fact, there is no depiction we can devise to describe our gods that is not applicable to each of us. The gods we create outside ourselves are a part of the same reality we exist in. The only edge they have over us is that we have given them power over us. For us to consider that we can be anything remotely like them is blasphemous and to think otherwise is to condemn ourselves to some place, again, we have created for those who compare their divinity to the divinity of their gods.

Thinking man has failed to recognize that, of all the devices ever made to generate, measure, or study energy, none comes close to the finely tuned instrument that *is man*. Man is made up of the same elemental forms, the same energetic qualities of the things he used to generate, measure, or study energy. Man is *one* with his creations, just as God is, and it is all energetic. It is all mysterious and wonderful beyond all imagining. The nature of man, just as with God, cannot be reasoned with. The thinking man, the mind of man, cannot comprehend the true complexity of man because it cannot see beyond the *not known*. It does not comprehend the *not known* nor can it. The reasoning or rational mind, as it is sometimes called, cannot see beyond a world of physical senses even though the human body, as an energetic and highly developed sensory device, is capable of *knowing* so much more.

Reasoning *takes in* that which comes from without through physical sensing and classifies those inputs based on historical inventory and reduces them to nothing more than what that inventory concludes, while inner knowing comes in the form of highly refined energetic knowing. The same as in me is the same as in all things. It is not knowing gained from sensing, categorizing, or preserving historical knowledge passed down generation to generation, but knowing on the same level as *being*. In other words, I am one with all, even, *I am one with all things*.

Only a quiet mind can see things in this way. Only a quiet mind can sense the oneness with all things. This kind of knowing is awareness and with this kind of awareness comes freedom. This kind of awareness frees the mind from needing the kind of inventory required to make so-called reasonable conclusions. It frees the mind and the body to be open to any possibility, indeed to accept any possibility. Freedom is born of awareness. Awareness is born of stillness. "Be still and know God." The quietness of the mind is where the voice of God is heard and the not known becomes known. God speaks to those who are still and the voice they hear is their own. This is not the voice of the mind that we all hear incessantly but a different voice, that while unique, is clearly our own. Hearing it shakes us to the very foundation of our souls only because we have not heard it before or if we have, we have not listened. When we hear this voice, it is with every energetic particle of our body and, unlike normal hearing, the cells and life forces that make us what we are sing a vibrating melody that cannot be mistaken for anything other than *knowing*. Every part of us is quickened and alive with new wondering and awe!

There is a paradox for man who is constantly thinking and looking for reason in the context of his thinking. His reason leads him to the very limits of the *unknown*, but prevents him from crossing that boundary since reasoning cannot go where it cannot find meaning in three- dimensional terms. Yet the *unknown* is always present, just around the next corner or bend in the road. The paradox is that the energy required to convince the mind of the soundness of its reason is all the energy needed to cross the border into the unknown. Spend it here or spend it there. The benefit is total freedom versus conditions. Reasoning prevents us from looking into the mysteries of God. Such mysteries are readily available to anyone who can still the mind, eliminate inventory, and learn to listen to the godlike sensing of energy. The still, small voice or whisperings of the spirit, whatever you may call it is the awareness of *oneness* with all things great or small, animate or inanimate. We can connect to that reality by stilling the mind.

What is really *out there* can never be known without the awareness of *in here*. What is *out there*, as perceived by our physical senses, is truly wondrous, but it is vastly limited to what is really there in the reckoning of reason which takes into account all our *reasonable* measures, such as time, space, distance, speed, sight, and sound, etc.

We cannot know how truly mysterious, incredible, and profound this world and all that is in it is. The reckoning of reason is not grand enough nor does it have the freedom to see beyond what it knows or reasons. It is in a cage from which it cannot escape without becoming small, in the sense that its knowing is nothing compared to its *not knowing*. Becoming small requires humbleness. Humbleness is the antithesis of ego. In other words, as conditioned as we are to seeing things the way we do, it would be extremely difficult to be humble enough to drive the ego out of existence. Difficult, but not impossible! Nothing is impossible. *Even a camel goes through the eye of a needle!*

How does one quiet the mind and drive out the ego? Quieting the mind takes awareness of the noise and chatter and vigilance and constancy. This is the same kind of vigilance and constancy used to make us the way we are now. From the moment of birth, and maybe even before that, we are constantly being told what to think or see or feel or sense. We are told so often over such a long time that we have become blind to anything else. We must constantly listen for the chatter and noise and stop it. With the same kind of constancy that got us to where we are now, we must do the same to remove our illusions and replace them with new knowing.

Being aware of the noise is half of eliminating it. Once we become attuned to the awareness of our chattering mind, we must repeatedly and constantly tell it to stop, or better, simply stop it. We can do this but as I mentioned earlier, it will be difficult. Mind chatter and noise have probably gone beyond the stage of habituation and are now part of our genetic make-up, our DNA. The cells of our bodies have given energy over to this chatter that has become the basis for our reason. Energy taken from cell tissue causes sickness and disease of both mind and body. Energy taken from cells in the body was never intended to be used to fuel egotistical desires and endless mind chatter. The ego is a glutton and will suck energy out of anything it can, including cell tissue. It sacrifices nothing of itself to stay intact, even allowing the destruction of its host, the physical body and mind that gives it life!

How often we hear now about the stresses of life causing serious illness and that lifestyle changes are necessary to preserve what is left. And what are the lifestyle changes we are asked to undertake when such diagnoses are pronounced? Slow down! Take a calmer approach to life and remove the stressful events and activities that have become the major part of our lives. Simply put, stress is noise and to overcome the effects of stress we need to quiet the noise. "Be still." Why does it take disease and a doctor's orders to recognize stress, or noise, for what it is? We all know this but we are so completely taken in by our illusions like our jobs, our financial security, our credentials, status, politics, education, and everything we care about that it takes a catastrophe or some form of suffering to jar us into considering that we have it all wrong. Our endless pursuit of the things in life that we have been conditioned to believe are important are not what really gives us peace, health, happiness, and abundance.

We must stop giving energy away to the incessant chatter of the mind and the insatiable appetite of the ego. Hear the mind thinking and stop it over and over again until it is silenced once and for all. The adage "one must lose his life to gain it" is what is meant by losing ego. The part of life we must lose is our egocentric identity that is known to the world. Jesus told his disciples "Let him deny himself," as if to say that anyone wanting to know his own divinity must give up the egotistical self. Denying oneself is not admitting, "I'm not me"; rather, it is recognizing that what we have projected to the world as "me" is not who or what we really are. What we are in the world is the mask we wear so that others accept us in the illusion we call "reality." What we show to the world is our way to fit in so that in the terms of the illusion, we are not looked at as nonconforming or strange. Denying oneself is to let go of all illusions created to find place in the world of illusion and simply be the *I am* that you are!

Egocentric identity is the weaver of webs, the teller of stories, and all the nooks and crannies of personality that culminate in making us who we want others to see us as. The ego is the judge and jury of all that goes on in the world as we know it. It is the embellisher, defender, and protector of all we have shown the world we are and it must be put aside. In order to have true life, the life of the ego must be lost. Denying oneself is to deny the false self we all put forward as *who we are* in a world that has been constructed to see only that false identity and would see the real identity as bizarre and off-the-wall. Jesus offered the *I am* forward as his only identity and he was despised by a majority of people because he did not fit in their world of illusion, their reality. In the last few hours of his life, even his disciples, the twelve who were with him through his three-year ministry, rejected him for fear of association with someone of such a strange identity. However, they were unable to *deny* themselves when the reality of their true identity caught hold of them. Jesus predicted that Peter would renounce him three times before the cock crowed and when the cock crowed, Peter must have finally understood how tied to the illusion he was because he went away and wept bitterly.

If anything, the story of the last few hours of Jesus' life illustrates how trapped all of us are in the egocentric devices of our minds and the reality that collectively our egos have created. It is not an easy thing to let go of all the things we have gathered to ourselves in this life that make us what we are and help us find place in it. We invest a lot of our energy maintaining our stories and making sure our place in the world, as we view it, holds up without too much disruption, embarrassment, or chaos. Reaching a point where we can accept that most of what we perceive in this reality is unimportant is the place where we begin to be able to lose the self importance we have been conditioned to believe is necessary to maintain our place in the world. This is the place where we take back our energy and in so doing, we can begin to know the true power, we as gods, possess. Then, like Jesus, we can perform the great miracles he said we could. As energetic beings, we are so much more than the egotistical mind can fathom and our true identity can only be known when we lose, or deny, the identity that everyone sees. *We spend our energy being what we are not or what we are.* We have the choice but knowing God only comes in denying the egocentric self that seeks place in a reality of illusion. Denying ourselves frees us from the illusion that squanders energy and buries us in an endless sea of noise and stress. Gods have no illusions!

Chapter 14

The Creative Process

It is not possible for something to be without *thinking* about it first. The difficulty about *thinking*, as it were, is that the first seed of thought is where all the power is. What we tend to do, however, is to continue to think about the original thought and start constructing the process by which we can realize it. In other words, we dilute the original thought with technicalities and mechanics that ultimately drain power from it.

No two creations are the same; however, a single thought is the *seed* of every creation. Creation comes with its own set of mechanics. Each original thought or *seed* will devise its own way and time to manifest itself in a *form* of its own choosing. In other words, our tendency to steer the construction of our thought into creative manifestation will only dilute and possibly frustrate the power of the creative process.

The creative process is very simple. We only make it complicated by attempting to second guess the mathematics each creation generates on its own. God proclaimed, "Let there be light!" and it was so. Simple! Think it, say it, and let it happen. That is the creative process. It is really that simple. God did not say, "Let there be light generated from a starlight source, say maybe that star out there. No, no, better yet, that star over there has whiter light and is a lot hotter, but if we put the planets out a little further, they'll be able to withstand the heat. However if they are further from the stars, it will take them longer to revolve around the sun which will mess up the timeline we have established for man to live a certain number of years based on a 365 day time cycle we need the human-compatible earth to circle the star. Oh, wait a minute. If we go to that star over there which is a white start like this one only bigger, it's gravitational pull will cause the planets to travel faster which just might be enough to speed their rotation to the 365 day time cycle. Oh, but wait! Because it's bigger, we have to put our habitable planet further away… Hmmm … Let me rethink this. Okay, okay, I've got it now. Maybe if we . . . ."

That is not how the creative process works. It requires thought only. Not thinking. It is a strange paradox: thought and thinking. A single thought carries the same creative energy as that by which worlds are formed or universes burst forth in the cosmos, and yet *thinking* carries enough energy as well to thwart the creative power of that single thought! Both have tremendous power and while the creative power of thought always manages to manifest something in our reality, the power of thinking takes it from the level of grandiose and spectacular to *this is all that is possible.* Thinking is usually coupled with our reasoning that through a lifetime of education, conditioning, and experience convinces us that our thoughts are unreasonable if they fall outside the bounds of the reasoning we have come to believe is all there is. Our conditioning teaches us to think within finite boundaries that literally rob the innate power of our thoughts of their true creative energy.

It is interesting that in speaking of the cosmos and the creation of galaxies or universes, scientists have coined the term "singularity" as the causal event preceding their bursting into existence. "Singularity" precedes creation and it might be thought of as the *single thought* that initiates each unique event in the universe. Every cosmic creation explodes into existence in its own way completely differently from any other in the universe, unique and wondrous from its own singularity. No two are ever the same, but each one is just as profound and spectacular as the next. So it is with thought. A single thought, undiluted and unanalyzed, carries the creative energy of any event in the universe. That single thought carries its own creative uniqueness and will manifest itself in incredible form, in unimaginable grandeur and beauty, if we leave it alone.

Thinking is a by-product of the fulfillment of previous thought. In other words, it is the result of coming to understand the rules, the mechanics or mathematics, by which previous creations came into being. The manifestation of a new creation carries its own science. Through observation, we can learn that *new* science and understand the laws which made it come to pass, but it will always only apply to that unique creation. We do not need to know nor can we know *how* things come to pass in the creative process. That is its beauty. Creation derived from a pure thought amasses energy and power from the ends of the universe and obeys only one simple principle — the principle of *what! What* is all any creative process needs to know and in its own processing the *how* will be made known, but only after we have realized the full creation of that unique thought.

The tendency to *think* about the *how* is perhaps the greatest distraction man has to overcome in the creative process. We are perceivers by nature and we are pathologically curious, a distraction, when it comes to the creative process. In this process, *thinking* becomes noise that prevents pure thought from forming and ultimately not materializing. Thinking is to thought as water is to soup. The more that is added, the more diluted it becomes. Thinking drowns out the creative energy from original thought and makes what is projected outward into the universe thin and weak and often with boundaries, limitations that the universe does not know until our thinking has presented them to it. *The creative power of the universe knows no bounds but thinking does!* If we but focus only on the *what*, the universe will give to us without any restrictions, rules, or limitations. That is how creation works!!

The process of thinking tends to blind us to *other* possibilities or realities because it is so wrapped up in our own ideas of reason. Our reasoning is the process we have developed that guides our thinking and we give ourselves up to it to such an extent that we lose our ability to dream and we end up challenging everything before us. Our reasoning leads us to accept only the reality we see or have adapted ourselves to. When we consider the infinite nature of the universe and how vast and wondrous we *as gods* are, how unfortunate that we let the mystery of *out there* become something finite and limited. Our reason does this to us because we have let it! Most of us think of ourselves as reasonable but it is our reasonableness that has closed us to the vastness of eternity. Our reasonableness presumes to have greater insight into what is creatively possible than the infinite universe of which we are a part. All our reason does is make more rigid our limited view of things, locking us in further to finite possibilities as opposed to the infinite. We are surrounded by infinity and unimagined grandeur that is only limited by the description we have accepted and *reasoned* is all there is. Our reasoning, which we like to think is expansive and impressive, is nothing in the realm of infinity but is powerful enough to close our minds to anything outside of it. Everything in our reality is upheld by our reason and anything that falls outside it is determined to be impossible or foolishness.

We start this process at birth and it continues throughout our lives. It is influenced initially by our parents and immediate family and extends out as we grow, taking in what some would call "archetypal" or "tribal" characteristics. These are the rituals or societal tendencies we develop: religious, political, educational, governmental, national, or whatever sensory inputs we are subjected to during any stage of our life. All of this information is analyzed, categorized, and used to formulate ultimately what we are. "As a man thinketh, so is he." What we are is a culmination of what we think about. Since thinking is built line upon line, it has a tendency to be chronological or historical, meaning that we develop our reasoning over time in sequential degrees someone or some institution has determined is just the right amount. We catalog events in such a way that supports such reasoning. As our reasoning becomes more refined and defined, it tends to become more and more dogmatic and judgmental, in the sense that we form unbreakable rules for ourselves and others that prevent us from seeing anything beyond these rules. We defend them vigorously to the point of anger or rage if they are violated. We use our historical data to defend our rules from attack or to convince others of their *rightness*. Our continuous thinking clutters our mind with what we believe is logic, evidence, rationalization and even more reasons, deepening our notion of *the rules* which have now taken on monumental proportions. Thinking is the process that ties us ever more strongly to only one reality, *ours,* and blinds us to an unlimited, infinite range of other possibilities.

Everything we see, perceive, believe, or think we know about anything in our range of thinking is nothing more than a *description* of what others believe or think they know it to be and have successfully convinced us of that same description. We can't see beyond what we have come to believe is *the way things are* because we are convinced by our *reason* that anything outside *that* description couldn't possibly be. And we will fight to defend that description because our thinking provides evidence of our reason every day and because we tend to be believers, we look out and see what we see and yes, it all fits our description. So it must be!

We must get back to the idea that everything we see or think we know is only a mere description of what is really there. We cannot get beyond our current description as long as we can only see that description. In fact, we will never come to any realization of our own *godliness* if we continue to see ourselves in our current description as *just* humans, sinners, good or evil, right or wrong, or whatever!

The truth is, what we see or think of the world in its current state is an illusion, and the majority of us are trapped in it and will remain trapped in it for the rest of our lives. That is how powerful *our* reason is. It literally blinds us to what we think really is and "what really is" is so much more than what we see or think we see, and certainly more than we know.

"Man's greatest limitation is *his own* ability to limit himself." Man's reasoning is just that—*man's reasoning*—and it is limited by his inability to hold a *thought* without *thinking* it into oblivion. Thought connects the finite to the infinite while thinking breaks that link! When we quiet the internal dialog that thinking and reasoning hold us in, that illusory world we're living in comes apart. We begin to see beyond what we perceive because now the inner part of our soul, based in the emotions, can sense beyond the chatter and noise of our thinking. Intuition is the language of gods. Gods hear, feel, see, touch and smell with finely tuned sensory instruments that cannot function in the noise of thinking minds, chattering, reasoning, and endlessly processing everything coming in through physical receptors.

How many times we've heard stories of scientists, inventors, writers, artists or what have you struggling for inspiration, clues, or answers to difficult problems only to have them come in moments of relaxation or sleep. With all the noise and chatter gone, the creator God we truly are bursts forth with incredible insight, creativity, simplicity, and detail the likes of which all our thinking, reasoning, and sensing could not begin to produce.

"I and my Father are one." We are the same. God resides with me, in me. I am God. He is me. I only need my physical being to be subjected to my spiritual to realize the true godlike power I possess.

This is difficult because *thinking* about what we constantly see or hear in the world of physical sensing, our world as we perceive it, convinces us over and over that what cannot be comprehended in this reality cannot possibly be either. The energy required to convince ourselves we are not gods is the very energy it would take to convince us that we are. Your thinking cannot focus on one thing and produce an opposite thought. *The energy required to convince us through thinking that we are less than we are will not suddenly produce a realization that we are greater than that thinking!* So how do we begin to accept our own divine or godlike nature? It's simple. Stop thinking about what you are not! *In fact, stop thinking!*

To stop thinking is to stop the endless chatter that *reasons* we are limited by *its* conditioned reasoning. It is not enough to say we must replace our current stream of thinking with opposite thinking because we are likely in the habit of it and very good at thinking the way we think. In fact, most of us believe our reasoning is so complete that we sometimes don't even know it, even when it is pointed out to us. It's almost as if our conditioning is grounded at the cellular level and every fiber of our bodies knows the limits of our conditioning, sometimes without thinking. The mind has to *shut itself up* so to speak. Every belief, religious or political, every idea about how things *are* in your world and all of the analysis that supports it must be quieted. Personal histories and all the stories we tell ourselves about every facet of life must be replaced with quiet, not opposite thought, but quiet. Noise and chatter is the workshop of egos. Quiet is the workshop of gods. The quiet mind is not an easy thing to come by since the ego loves noise, glitz, fanfare, excitement, and attention.

Look at the world in which we live. Everything the mind of man has done or is doing supports the stimulation the ego craves. Ego craves noise. It pursues it with aggressiveness in an endless need to nourish itself and anything blocking its source of life and voracious appetite is crushed in a clamor of even more noise. Subtly the ego will even let opposite thoughts enter the stream of thinking in order to convince you that such a method of continuous thinking is necessary, and so our thinking will change from current ideas and developed education, what have you now, to that of "Oh yes, I really am great" or "I am a god." Oh yes, all of it is true and here is why. It will take you down that road of chatter and noise because ego does not care where the drama or story of life comes from as long as it can feed itself with a story of some kind that brings attention to it. Ego is subtle in its deception. Thought, in its purest form, is the creative process. Thinking foils it. Ego knows this. Thought carries with it its own *how*, and it doesn't require the *hows* of that thought to understand anything about that *how*. It simply requires the *knowing* that within that pure thought it will manifest itself, in its own way and time.

Thinking, on the other hand, carries its own *how*, *why*, *when*, or *where*. Thinking cannot get the attention it requires if it accepts that a simple thought carries its own *how* and so it begins a process of questioning, reasoning, and manipulation that drains energy and dilutes the original thought. It is part of the baggage that thinking uses to resolve complex desires it cannot accept in simple terms. So it looks for logical explanations which typically end up concluding that the *thought* cannot become reality.

Thinking creates inventory, an inventory of broken ideas, hopes, dreams and any number of historical perspectives that arise now and then and are rehashed based on current triggers or new information making them worthy of more analysis. Just as items gathered and stored for years fill and clutter once empty space in the basement or attic of our homes, so too does the mind fill with these inventories of thoughts, analysis, and conclusions formulated over long periods of thinking and processing. Years and years may go by before anything comes along to trigger the inventoried thought, but the mind kicks into high gear trying to recover all the data and conclusions so it is ready to respond with the precision all that past thinking created. The mind is activated and processing, absorbing energy and time. The more inventory carried in the mind, the more likely everyday occurrences will prompt the mind to begin rummaging through endless files of unused data. The more energy expended, the less likely it is for the mind to quiet itself so as to hear the whisperings of the inner self. The god within is overridden with the noise generated from endless thinking.

The god within is always present, always aware, and always whispering but not in the loud, overbearing way of the mind. It is the still, small voice all of us hear sometimes. If you are able to recall those moments when the voice of God is heard, it is always in a time of heightened awareness. Perhaps by natural occurrence, you come near to death, or you are with a loved one who is very ill and you simply have no other option than to let things be just as they are. No judgments, or sadness, or even happiness, just presence and all the noise of the mind is silent and nothing but the warm calm of existence, your awareness of existence, is all there is. You are "cool, calm, and collected," as they say, and nothing but presence and stillness bathes your existence. In that moment, you know God. You know oneness with who you really are and it is as if the world stands still. At that moment, every physical sense, and every biological process has ceased to exist. You are no longer aging because time has stopped. You are caught up in the infinite, an infinite ocean of awareness. You simply know all that is necessary to exist in this moment. The mind is quiet, thinking has ceased, and you swim endlessly in the calm stillness of inner silence, inner awareness—the still, small voice of God.

It is in this place that true *knowing* exists. This is where the knowing that "Ye are gods" exists. It is hard to accept because most of us hardly ever go there. It's hard to get there amidst the noise we are accustomed to and the effort we exert to function in our otherwise sensory world. There is a lot coming in through our senses and the thinking nature of the mind is constantly trying to reconcile those inputs to its own already formed conclusions about the reality it has created.

We all know intuitively that there is a lot more going on than what we take in through our physical senses. Scientists have demonstrated over and over that within the world we know through physical sensing, so much more is going on. There are incredible, wondrous things that escape all possible description and understanding and yet we *accept* them as though there is nothing more than that which our mind has comprehended through physical sensing and thinking can reasonably sort out. In reality, the physical senses are like a cage in which we have placed ourselves. The bars of the cage are so real and so strong that we can't break out of them. At some point we stop trying as if the bars (our senses) break us of what we intuitively know and our own science confirms.

Even in those pristine moments of infinite awareness, when the bars built by our senses have been completely removed, we quickly reconstruct them around us, like an animal caged all of its life is afraid to leave the area of the cage even when it has been removed. Or afraid to venture out even when it has been freed of the physical restraints that once held it captive.

That cage becomes our world and even if we remove all the restraints and bars from it, our conditioning is so profound that we keep ourselves confined. That is what we have done in creating our particular description of the world. That description consists of all the things we have been told and taught repeatedly until that description is so strong that we no longer look past it, or even consider that it is just a description that works for us in three-dimensional terms.

Thinking does this to us. The continuous chatter of dos and don'ts, yeses and nos, rights and wrongs, compounded over and over until our own imaginary boundaries trap us in a world that is completely limited but only because we have allowed it to be so. We have permitted it to take form in our life and so we must ourselves change it. It's a hard thing to do. Few have ever been successful in achieving this to the extent that they fully realize their own god-like nature. That is how profound and pervasive the conditioning becomes over a lifetime.

In the New Testament, Peter came close when he too walked on water, but in the noise of his mind, he lost it! His mind probably repeatedly challenged him to question what was happening *now* with what he had always known from past thinking and education. "How could you possibly walk on water now, when in all of life experience to now, you have never done it, nor have you known anyone who has done it? It can't be done, so what do you think you are doing?" Surely these thoughts or other thoughts like them were going through his mind as he stood on the water and so powerful were they that they convinced him that he could not walk on water even though he was in the act of doing it. He had actually experienced it and something took him over, caused him to lose his belief, and he began to sink. That is how powerful our conditioning and reason is. Even in the act of actually doing something wonderful, mysterious, and supposedly impossible we let our conditioning, our reason, pull us back to where it has always said we belong. The description we form for ourselves is massive, impressive, and formidable, and it continues to reinforce itself through everyday observation and confirmation. It never stops looking for proof of its reasonableness!! The world we uphold by our reason becomes a series of events and circumstances we continuously analyze and file away to support any and all intrusions that would tell us otherwise.

Yet stopping the chatter and breaking the bonds of a lifelong description is exactly what must be done. We must work to convince ourselves that regardless of any logic, our description has "all things are possible" within it. "All things are possible!!" In a subtle but deceptive way, we have allowed our description of reality to dilute our belief that "all things are possible" into something more like "all things that *are* possible *are possible* to him that believeth." In other words, our reasoning has convinced us that all things are not possible save only what our reasonableness has convinced us is and only that is possible! It is not the case. All things are possible and our power to create anything is limitless by any condition or precept we, through our description, have come to accept.

Again, we must quiet the mind. Stop thinking and start listening to our higher selves. We must release ourselves from everything within any realm of attention. This includes histories, relationships, work worries, obligations, health, position, differences, disagreements, hurts, or anything we believe has been done to us by others. This includes nearly everything that can connect our identity to anything outside our selves and everything as we know it. Within this encompasses anything that causes argument, justification, or reasoning of any kind in the mind. All our stories, beliefs, and routines must be removed from the active part of our thinking processes and we must convince ourselves that something greater and more profound exists, and is not confined to the limits of our thinking or beliefs. Everything must be reduced to a level of insignificance that removes all need of judgment.

It is almost like accepting everything that is, but also everything that isn't. It sounds contradictory but if you consider how long it has taken to condition us to the way we are, it will take the same kind of conditioning to open us up to the kind of awareness that accepts all things and see all things as beautiful and wondrous. It takes a quiet, neutral mind to do this because every prejudice we carry with us contains the seed of noise and disagreement. It is in stillness that the voice of God speaks to us and it is always succinct and without reason, whys, or wherefores. What remains is just pure simple thought and all the creative possibilities of an infinite universe opens to us and nothing is impossible!

Chapter 15

Forgiveness

Forgiveness only exists because we judge when we have been specifically asked not to. In other words, judgment always precedes any act or cause where an outcome requires forgiveness and all outcomes where we feel we have been wronged require forgiveness. It is difficult to comprehend as humans why we are asked to give away the pain or hurt we have suffered at the hands of others and yet when we consider the idea that forgiveness is a *giving away of the burden of carrying pain and hurt,* it should begin to be apparent that giving up pain and hurt would be a good thing to do. Most of us wallow in our hurt. We personalize it, allow it to permeate our being, and remind anyone who will listen of the suffering we underwent at the hands of whomever. It is as if the pain and hurt assumes its own identity and attaches itself to us in such a way that we are forever reminded of the offense against us. Over the course of a lifetime, this can add up to an incredible burden of weight and the mental or energetic strain, for some, is more than they can bear.

Incredibly, long after the initial hurt, we continue to feel the weight of such acts to the extent that all the emotions of resentment, anger, embarrassment, or whatever type they may be are triggered at the slightest provocation. Sometimes we become emotionally charged and cannot pinpoint exactly what it is that is causing such feelings and those who witness such outbursts are left wondering why such triggers caused so much emotion and upheaval. Sometimes it hardens both in such a way that body and spirit are broken under the weight. Some go to their graves bitter and angry with the sting of emotion as alive as it was all those years ago when the whole incident that sparked so much internal angst occurred, perhaps having taken all of ten minutes out of an entire lifetime. *What infraction is worthy of a lifetime of anger and bitterness?* Sometimes the bitterness and anger is carried over from generation to generation, giving life to something that should never have had life to begin with. Parents would rather set their own children's "teeth on edge" and condemn them to a life of bitterness, anger, and struggle than to give it up and release themselves and their posterity from the original wounds. Again, it is the score keeping nature of ego that makes sure all injustices keep their place in a sort of *unforgiven hall of fame!*

Forgiving is rarely described as giving up the wounds of some original act. It is typically described as something of epic proportion with the fate of nations resting on an outcome that will literally invoke nations to war with each other if we give up our reasons to hold on to it. How absurd! All because of an offense *judged* to be worthy of such remembrance that occurred who knows how long ago, and took minutes to transact! Imagine the expense of energy holding such things within our minds and keeping both the emotion and feelings bundled up inside to be expressed when the appropriate time and place presents itself. Precious, precious energy dispensed on things that are of no importance to gods but ever important to ego. Why do we do it?

When we step away from these infractions, look at them for what they are, and consider them in the light of "How do they affect me as to my own spiritual growth," the answer is almost always "They don't." How could they? Consider, again, that there is no right or wrong and that the acts of others can only hurt or offend us because we allow it. The only part of us that gets offended or hurt over anything is the egocentric side of us and it is only the rules ego has imposed that are broken. No sin is ever committed! In fact, this may be one of the most obvious indicators of how strong our ego is when seemingly every little thing finds a way to hurt or offend us. We even see individuals become martyrs with the weight of national consciousness on their frail shoulders over things and events that happened decades, even centuries before. How is it that anything is worthy of such sacrifice? We are not meant to be this way and certainly gods are not. Gods cannot be hurt because everything that happens is a part of the wondrous beauty of existence and all of it is just good. There is never an upside or downside because in infinity, choices do not exist. Events are nothing more than *events* and to carry such things upon us as if they mattered in an infinite spectrum of possibilities is to needlessly waste energy on things that cannot possibly affect us unless we allow it. This is a paradox in life that exists because of conditioning we inherit from birth and continues on throughout our lives but it does not need to be this way. Along the way we take on the causes of others and our own, making the burden even greater and greater. All because we cannot see past the idea of opposites in the world and in that narrow perspective we are consigned to judge the better of those opposites. Jesus somehow knew this and was aware that there is no way out of the conditioning to judge we undergo from birth other than with *new* conditioning. *Forgiving is the new conditioning that replaces the old conditioning of judging.*

It is incredibly difficult to forgive, however, in light of the sheer number of judgments we hold to be absolute and final, we must do it if we are ever going to shed the weight of years and years, even generations and generations of begrudging, anger, and suffering we carry in our minds and on our backs. This is the losing of life to find it that Jesus speaks of, more specifically replacing the old with the new. In the Old Testament, God is jealous, vengeful, and full of wrath in response to the acts of His children. In the

New Testament, He is forgiving, kind, and loving. What changed? God did not transform; only our description of Him did. We must alter our own description as well! We must shed the old life of judgments, and replace it with a life that recognizes that no act is sinful and that we must forgive everyone of every act we find offensive until we are washed clean of the old ways and are dressed in the new. Forgiveness is the way to new life, new meanings, and new awareness!

Jesus said that we must forgive everyone of everything regardless of how large the offense our judgment has deemed it to be. It is not that forgiveness is a requirement to achieve heavenly status or a predicate to becoming perfect or god-like. It is necessary because we *judge* and in judging, we limit ourselves to the fullness of our creative and infinite abilities. Forgiveness provides us a way through our suffering and a mechanism for overcoming the burdens we carry upon ourselves because we have judged. It is a way to get back to living life from inward to outward. Judging requires us to look outward at the actions of others instead of looking inside at ourselves. "Judge not that ye not be judged," the words state. Why these words? Why the question? Why the exhortation to "not judge"? Isn't everything in life a judgment of one thing or another? It is but it should not be. Again, we were given to know good and evil but never were we assigned to be the judges of it. *There is no sin where there are no judgments,* but most of us in our conditioned state of judging do not get that there is no sin or that evil does not exist in the world, universe, or anywhere else.

Because there is no sin, there is no need to judge the acts of others against any criteria but we have all been conditioned another way. We all judge and in so doing we carry tremendous burdens of pain, guilt, sorrow anger, and so much more in our souls. Where there is no judgment, there is no need for forgiveness. So why the command to forgive?

We are all raised to *see* things in a certain way and from our view, we believe that our perspective is the only *seeing* that has validity. Such a validity, narrowly defined, supposes that everyone should *see as we see*. The seeing we rigidly adhere to is not seeing, however. It is judging. This is the very thing we are commanded not to do! Judgment is the eyes we have all been conditioned to see through to one degree or another, but it limits the field of view we are capable of truly perceiving as divine beings. Additionally, judgment creates a competitive element or duality in everything we see or do. This then becomes the basis that defines our seeing or acting as being *better* than or *worse* than someone else's seeing or acting. Yet our conscious awareness, the eyes we currently see through, demands that we choose *something* over *anything* else.

Gods do not choose the better of available choices. They act knowing that all choices are the right choice in the realm of infinity. In this human existence, we choose between this or that, but in so choosing nothing more is required--that is all we are asked. *Choose* this or that and then act. We need not analyze the choice as to whether it is good or bad. Act deliberately and purposefully but only as *you* have chosen, and no more. In other words, there *is* only *one* way to do anything and it is uniquely *your* way and no one else's. It is uniquely without judgment of any kind and it is all yours, but yours only. As far as this life is concerned, every so-called, choice we make is the correct one and no God will stand in judgment. Judging brings into play the idea that "someone" is the ultimate arbitrator and that in so judging, that choice is best for everyone. Consider why there is so much venom between opposing factions whether they be political, religious, national, ethnic, or what have you? It is not that one side is right and the other is wrong. It is that one side claims that in their rightness every other opposing view is wrong and that is simply not the case. It is the judgment that produces the angst. Impose no judgment and the venom disappears. Disagree with an opposing view but don't judge it right or wrong. If you are offended, forgiveness is your way to freedom and the loss of burdensome feelings of anger, frustration, embarrassment, and shame. If you offend, forgiveness is likewise your way to freedom. How often do we see individuals who have committed offensive acts against others only to beat themselves up endlessly over it? Forgiveness is required here as well.

In order to overcome our conditioned judgmental selves, we must repeatedly forgive and forgive and forgive. We must replace our conditioning to judge with the conditioning that no need for judgments exists. We do so through the act of forgiveness. Forgiveness heals us and lifts the burden of painful scars incurred over a lifetime of unnecessary judgments that in the true light of day never meant anything anyway.

You are the *maker*. You own your life and no others. Make your choices, but impose nothing on anyone or anything. Make you choices but do not judge them as good or bad. None of that matters. Take any form of judgment out of the process and our clarity of focus and the view in front of us widens and sharpens and life rolls on in abundance and splendor. Everything becomes good and wondrous and your life, no matter what happens, is beautiful, rich, and full. What we see through non-judgmental eyes becomes more vast, spacious, and awesome. Everything becomes a part of everything else and what we once judged as good or evil now becomes a necessary piece of the whole experience we now enjoy. Instead of being filled with anger, hurt, and pain, we are overflowing with abundance and the wonderment of life like we never knew possible.

Letting go requires forgiveness. This is not the "I can forgive but not forget" kind of forgiveness we hear some say. We must forgive and forget at a very deep level of consciousness. Holding on to thoughts of pain or hurt incurred from the acts of others is reason for the mind to justify its pain or hurt. Pain and hurt are a heavy load none of us need carry; bearing it for any length of time is a needless indulgence that drains our energy and the energy of others. Forgiving releases us from the need to have unnecessary conversation and dialog internally about events. The actions of others or ourselves that caused us to judge those acts and events only adds more to the already endless chatter of the mind. This kind of dialog, along with all the other things our minds constantly play over and over, is noise and the kind of chatter that keeps us stuck in our present state away from the wonder of what life really holds for us. We are gods! *We should see as gods!*

Free yourself from the noise of justification but when the conditioning of life that led you to judge overwhelms you and you pass unnecessary judgment, forgive and be forgiven. Let the infinity of the universe and your innate nature as gods absorb the finite reason of judgments old and new. Give them up for the sweet balm of forgiveness that unyokes us from all the insignificant events we have held so near and dear to us. Release them and judge no more for nothing is wrong! Whatever the events of our lives are, regardless of our particular walk of life, everything is for our good! Life has a peculiar way of opening up to us only those things that can do us good. Even those things that we see as dark and treacherous are there as beautiful gems to be gathered to us. Everything in life enriches us if we choose to find those gems and take from them all the beauty they hold for us. Bask in the new found energy that comes from opening the doors and letting all the judgments flow out and *new life flow in!* Do not be seduced into finding cause to ever judge again, but if you must, work to make forgiveness the foundation of your life. *Again, nothing in this existence can hurt you!* You are gods and gods are not besought with the unimportant barbs of others. Be impenetrable. Throw off the old life of judgment and resentment and take on the new that sees life through eyes that have been cleansed and cleared through forgiveness! *Indulge* only in life and all of its wondrousness and beauty; accept that everything life offers is just a part of an infinite spectrum of possibilities. Breathe all of it in as fully as you can. Live life as the gods do. Bask in your infinity. Be the *divinity* that you are.

Forgiveness is the doorway to Heaven. *Open it and be free!*

Chapter 16

The Intuitive Life

We live in paradox. We are spiritual beings living in a three-dimensional life consisting of energetic forms of every kind. Spirit surrounded by form, yet all of it spiritual and made up of energetic matter no different from anything else and yet the form we see around us is so real, solid, and definable by the language of our minds. In other words, we consist of the same energy as everything we see on this earth or in every other universe, but we are trapped by the limitation of our thinking and language to describe anything as it really is.

What really *is* transcends anything we perceive with our five senses. Yet the five senses are so certain and rigid about what is there and our thinking and language have been shaped to support those perceptions even though at every level of our being we intuitively know greater things are a part of our reality. Seeing anything beyond the five senses is difficult because of the conditioning we have all undergone in a lifetime of institutional learning, societal acceptance, and family traditions. What our physical senses cannot comprehend is the infinite nature of all things in existence. For the most part, infinity is a *long, long time*. We can't seem to get beyond the idea of time and yet in the realm of infinity there is no time. Time is a construct of man's thinking to give chronological order to the events of life and to place in reference all of our history, both individually and collectively. As energetic beings, we are timeless and to try to make our thinking mind construct an accurate picture of what that means is, again, trying to define the infinite with the finite. It cannot be done using three-dimensional communication techniques.

Energy is infinite and so are we. Our form is a mass of energy that has coalesced into the physical structure we call the body. While the body is sophisticated and complex, when it is broken down it is a vibrating sea of energy just like everything else on our planet. Energetically, we are identical to everything whether we see it or not. Energy is everywhere and so are we. Energy is with or without form and so are we. The light from distant stars is energy and so are we. There is no such thing as *difference* when we speak about anything in energetic terms. All things are equal in the context of energy regardless of how or what form that energy has taken. There is no *apart* from. All things are equal.

Just as all things are equal, so too are all things connected. We literally are one, more precisely one with everything that ever was, is, or will be. In energetic terms, everything we see in this three-dimensional universe is an integrated part of the same whole. When we speak of roots, we literally have roots in the very existence of everything we see and don't see, not just our family, religious, or cultural heritage. Everything in existence is the same as us and lives energetically in such a way that we can know it other than intellectually or through the means of our five physical senses. Energy lives and that which lives, speaks and that which speaks, communicates.

Energy has a language. It is the language of vibration and we all vibrate to the dialog contained within our current vibrating form whether it be human, animal, water, mineral, etc. The speed at which all things vibrate is all that separates us from speaking the language of all the forms that have taken shape around us. The language of energy, and thus of all things, is vibration. Even our five senses are receptors of vibration that have been highly refined and tuned to the reality of this physical dimension we live in. Our eyes see light vibration. Our ears hear sound vibration. When we touch something, we can sense warmth or coolness or pressure, all of which are energetic vibrations relayed back to our brain and interpreted in the forms and constructions we know as this reality but all of it, including the electrical impulses that transmit information to the brain, are vibrational. Vibration is the language of energy and as energetic beings, we are capable of perceiving so much more than we do through the five senses.

Most of us at one time or another have felt the presence of some other form or entity near to us, or have thought we could communicate with the trees or animals or nature. It is not understood how this takes place; it just simply is. Perhaps some have communicated with such things in a way they can only understand or know. Everything in the universe lives and all things teem with life and knowing that, in reality, we are a part of it all. That with which we are a part is also that with which we communicate. Whether we know it or not, everything in existence radiates it own essence and vibrating signals that everything else in existence is in tune with. Our bodies recognize this and we intuitively know that we are connected to all things in physical and spiritual ways, although we as humans have the unique ability to turn it off. We turn it off by drowning it out with the noise of thinking, ego, and five-sensory awareness. We turn it off by trying to find terms in our own language that explain it even though there are none. The language of energy is vibration and, so, to speak to other forms, we must learn to *hear* vibration and adjust our own to be able to communicate with all the other forms in our reality. This is the intuitive life. Living life energetically is to have another awareness of it that is not gated with limitation such as the five senses. Living life energetically is living intuitively.

Intuition is the device all humans have to communicate with the vibrations going on all around us and exceeds all the other three-dimensional, sensory means of communication. It is the hearing that comes from not hearing with our ears or the seeing that comes from not seeing with our eyes. It is *knowing* at a deeper level of understanding, a "vibrational" level rather than the human sensory level. It is the unfiltered communication of the infinite that hears no *other* voice. Intuition is the language of gods. It is the sudden knowing of something for no apparent reason at all other than "something spoke and my body heard and every cell of my body simply knew." Some people have premonitions or a sixth sense, as it is sometimes called, when a loved one passes on, or someone they are close to is hurt or needs them. Most of us have experienced similar feelings of this kind of knowing. It is knowing at a different level than the five physical senses allow for. It is vibration or intuitive knowing that we all possess. Most of us have simply forgotten how to use it or have allowed the noise of the other senses to drown it out so it has little or no impact in our lives.

Some claim to have the *gift* of intuition, but intuition is not a gift. It may seem like a gift to some because they may be *tuned in* at a higher level than others, but as energetic beings, we all speak some vibration. The equipment associated with vibration might not work very well but only because of a lack of use. The overt nature of our physical senses and the tendency of our thinking to align with three-dimensional reality to the exclusion of everything else is why most of us have lost this ability to speak or hear by means of vibration.

The intuitive life sees beyond physical sensing and knowing. It is plugging into life through vibration and reconnecting with the energetic forms we have systematically excluded from our current three-dimensional reality. It is perceiving all things as one and the same and it is also understanding the infinite nature of everything. Intuition is the only way we can know anything outside our physical senses, yet it is the greatest communicative tool we possess. We must embrace our intuitive nature in order to fully recognize our godlike nature and to be able to communicate with everything in existence. Intuition is the way we detach ourselves from the illusions of our current reality and stop expending our energy on things that are of our own construction. Put another way, our three-dimensional reality keeps us focused on all the things that support that reality never letting us look outside at what is really there but can only be known intuitively.

Intuition bears a resemblance to the things of this reality. It never looks like fear or foreboding or the other emotional triggers we have developed throughout our lives. All of the so-called emotions such as sadness, happiness, fear, anger, jealousy, and all the others are often confused with intuitional knowing but intuition knows no emotion. It is unbiased *knowing* that comes from another place from within and permeates the entire body in a calm assurance that dispels all doubts. Emotions are good monitors that the actions we take are good, but they should not be mistaken for intuitive insight. Emotions are physical extensions of our thinking. In other words, we may be thinking or doing something that makes us happy or excited and we wear that emotion on our physical countenance. Others can plainly see that we are happy or excited and indeed we feel it on a very physical level. Likewise, all the so-called emotions express themselves in a physical way to the extent that we can identify *how we feel*. We perceive sadness, anger, hurt, jealousy, fear and all the other emotions as physical expressions of what we or someone else is doing or thinking. The difference between intuition and emotion is that intuition never carries emotion. Intuitive insights carry certainty and with that certainty there is an assurance that comes from a place of stillness that knows none of the emotional expressions manifested physically. It is possible to have an emotion express itself once the intuitive insight becomes known to the thinking mind and in such cases, the mind convinces the body to feel or to express the appropriate emotion.

For example, I have always had a sense of other realities and indeed the awareness of the presence of other entities not of this reality. I have always had trouble understanding such awareness or knowing, so emotionally I have always equated these experiences as something to fear and my reaction physically has been to hide under the covers, close my eyes, tremble, or get as far away from the sensation as I could. That is the way I reacted emotionally to such events that have happened off and on throughout my life. In fact, I classified such encounters as the presence of evil and quite naturally, such a description would evoke the reaction of fear or dread in me. One occasion, however, and many more since then, I was walking from one end of the house to another in the dark when I felt a hand press itself on my right shoulder blade. It wasn't a slap, friendly pat, or a grabbing of the shoulder to halt me or spin me around. It was just a gentle touch of a hand on my shoulder blade. At the physical level, I froze in fear as I had so many times before and my mind instantly focused on all the things I must do to be rescued from this affront. I was terrified and my mind was doing what it has always done so well. Run, scream, pass out, wet yourself, shiver and shake, fall to the floor in the fetal position, quiver until this passes, and so on! For some reason, however, amidst the noise of my incessant mind an intuitive insight came to me that I was in no danger. It wasn't an audible voice but a strong sensation emanating from deep within my body that carried with it a great sense of calm and peace. At that instant, all fear left me and for a few seconds I was calm, unafraid, and a sweet peace embraced me. I turned around to face this entity knowing with absolute certainty that I was in no danger whatsoever. As I turned, I saw the faintest outline of a figure that was probably four to six inches taller than me (I'm six foot, two inches tall) and while I was unable to distinguish any other characteristics other than the outline, I knew I was in the presence of someone benevolent and kind who was only there to make himself known to me in the form I beheld. I asked the entity, "Who are you?" but there was no reply either to my physical senses or to my intuitive knowing. All that was happening was all that was going to happen. Nothing was spoken or going to be spoken at that time; however, my mind had kicked back up with all of its reasoning and chatter that I needed to exit and exit quickly!

The voice of the mind is powerful and coupled with its instruction to the various glands in the body to secrete hormones that make us tense up, shiver, shorten our breath, what have you. I fought through all the stress and anxiety of my mind expressing itself physically and emotionally and stood there looking at the entity determined not to cower as I had always done before. I know that I had heard the intuitive voice and I felt the calm assurance that swept over me and that only comes with *knowing* that I was in no danger. I fought through the fear and stayed and faced that entity without words or expressions of any kind until it quietly turned and walked away, eventually fading into the darkness. At that moment, I again felt the release of emotional stress, fear, anxiety, and a wave of warm assurance confirming my original intuitive insight that I was in no danger swept over me. The whole encounter lasted about fifteen minutes but I felt great!! It was unlike anything I had felt prior.

We live in parallel worlds. One holds the egocentric identity we have created that is recognizable in our three-dimensional world. It is the world in which thinking and emotion have place and our reality lies almost solely in the domain of what we perceive through the five physical senses and our emotional responses to them. This reality is tied very strongly to our physicality and all the sensory inputs we receive every day are stored in our minds for reference. It is a reality grounded in the advancement of time and the vastness of space. Past and future events are our main focus as if to say we are always focused back on something from our past or forward to something in our future. The second world is our true self or infinite nature that we rarely come to know. It is the world of knowing the unknown and of hearing the voice of that true self. The voice of true self is the voice of intuition. Intuition is never grounded in time and space. In fact it might be said that time stands still and that space, which we have always believed to be empty, is suddenly abundant and full of indescribable wonder. When we hear the intuitive voice, time always stops and *being* as we know it ceases to be. For those brief insightful moments, we no longer age and a hundred years of time, knowledge, and wonderment can be compressed into a few short seconds and in that brief time we are enriched and enlightened like never before. Infinity requires something greater than physical sensing to be comprehended and intuition, the voice of god, is the mechanism we all possess to help us do it. While thinking, emotion, and ego tie us to opposites and judgments, intuition does not. The voice of God is pure, simple, and sweet. It is a voice we all have within us! We all know that voice but have let the noise and chatter of the thinking mind drown it out. Intuition is the way we commune with the infinite and find our place with it. It is always present time and the phenomenon of time and space cease to function as *what is now is all there is and all there is going to be.* "Take no thought for tomorrow" were the words of Jesus. Present time is where gods live and it is where we hear their voices.

Since everything is infinite, the intuitive life does not judge one thing to be good and another bad. Infinity is a scale which is incomprehensible to the three-dimensional thinking of man, yet man thus limited is constantly trying to comprehend it, and ultimately the endless chatter that goes with it. The concepts of good and bad or any form of judgment does not make sense on a scale of infinity. Where do you put either on such a scale? Where do you put judgments of any kind? Infinity absorbs everything that has meaning in the egotistical experience of this life and dilutes any importance we place on the things or events of life.

On the three-dimensional plane, we need to consider that death hunts us. Death is just around the corner for each of us and in a life where death is inevitable, the same things and events that get lost in infinity should also lose importance. Death comes too soon for us to live anything but an intuitive life. It has also been said that death is the great equalizer because we will all die, but it really is not. The only true equalizer for all things is infinity. Death is just a possibility in the world of the infinite, just as life is and regardless of how actions are viewed and labeled, they are nothing more than the infinite possibilities available to all of us. The events of life are simply the makeup of infinity with all things equal, but different. "Different," however, must not be viewed in terms of opposites or as choices we make because we judge one thing better than the other. "Different" here means in the sense of *abundance,* both of possibility and opportunity.

The intuitive life is a life of doing. There is not enough time to live with worry, fear, and doubt as far as this three-dimensional life is concerned. Nothing we have to worry about or fear compares to our passing out of this life and into the infinite existence from whence we came. Nothing is more serious than living life abundantly, and yet our egocentric mind places such great importance on its own preservation, identity, and stature that everything it attracts to itself is worrisome or stressful in some way or another. Worrying about our decisions after making them is, again, placing importance on something that has no significance in infinity and pales in comparison to our own infinity. Why do it? Why live in such a way when to live intuitively we act as the gods and move forward with the assurance that every step of the way is accountable to life. *Not just our life but all of life!*

Intuitive living is clearer because we act from an inner knowing that is made without balancing between good or bad, or better or best. The intuitive person knows that any decision is just that — any decision. It does not carry any *what if* concerns nor can it be questioned afterwards as to whether it was right or wrong or good or bad. There's no time for such consideration nor would it matter if there were. Each decision carries its own power to act and requires no assessment of its relative value to anyone or anything past, present, or future. There is only a series of *nows*, within which each decision is made. The *now* is where the action begins and each *now* is the action carried through. No regrets, no sadness, no remorse. The journey is too great and the road too awesome and wondrous for any of these things.

The intuitive life cuts through the delusional aspects of our ego identification and the sensory description of what we believe we know about every aspect of life and our world. The intuitive life perceives the vibration of all things animate or inanimate and simply knows and acts with the understanding that no act is greater or less than any other. In other words, no act that is intuitively struck upon is wrong. Nor is it right. It simply *is* a moment in present time that has penetrated our thinking and settled into the greater depth of our soul as if we have been spoken to by an angel.

The intuitive individual lives every day, every minute by knowing the *not known*. The *not known* can only be heard through the language of energy, or vibration. Energetic vibration cannot be heard through the noise and chatter of the thinking mind. It is the still, small voice that is sometimes spoken of. Those solemn moments, sometimes thought of as inspiration, are where for whatever reason the noise of mind is quieted and that sweet gift of knowing burst through, often to our surprise and wonderment. "Where did that come from?" we ask. Intuition is always there. It is *still* and *small* because we, through our three-dimensional reasoning, have made it so.

Intuition connects us to infinity of which we are all a part. It is the key to understanding what unlocks the mystery without which we could never comprehend anything outside the physical senses. Without intuition we are left thinking how insignificant and small we are because three-dimensional knowing has to include time and space and our place within it. When we look at time and space through our three dimensional-senses, we lose the connection to infinity that intuition lets us comprehend. Intuition has no filters. It operates at a cellular level. Some say it operates at an atomic or quantum level which may be the case. Intuition is vibrating energy that is not comprehended at the level of our physical senses. The egotistical filters we pass everything through are not fine enough to detect the ever present intuitive voice. It is only when we bring the intuitive voices forward into our three-dimensional awareness that the ego kicks in and then tries to apply its reason to what we are given to know through intuition. Only we can regulate the filters of ego, by stopping or allowing the analysis and judgment of the knowing that comes to us through the intuitive voice so we must be vigilant and quiet the mind when the noise of thinking, analyzing, and egocentric reasoning starts in on an intuitive insight.

The intuitive voice is almost always the first voice we hear although it usually is not a voice at all but a feeling or premonition, but it is always clear and unfiltered. Whatever it is, we all have felt it and whatever way best describes how it comes to us or how we feel when it does is unimportant as long as we know that is what it is. We all experience it in different ways, but we almost always know what it is. Sometimes we may know what someone is about to say before they say it, or sense something not quite right about a particular situation, or we get nudged to turn a certain direction, or enter a building, or go talk to someone for no particular reason. We could go on and on about the multitude of ways in which the intuitive knowing we all possess manifests itself, but it is rarely relevant in our lives, only because we have forgotten and masked how relevant it is. Most of us have become so confident through the conditioning, of our five-sensory awareness that intuitive sensing has been relegated to the realm of sorcery, the paranormal, or oddity. Most of all, intuition has been questioned by some because to act intuitively requires an act of will that comes without any reason or *how to*. It takes will to act on intuitive insight! Listening to the intuitive voice requires acceptance that what follows *will* take care of itself and this is nearly impossible to do for the reasoning mind. This is a difficult thing to ask a highly structured egotistical mind that thinks it can come up with a better *knowing* out of its finite repertoire of possible steps and outcomes. The mind loves the noise of its accumulated reason and finds security in the limited knowledge it has acquired. When it has no basis upon which to conduct an analysis, it resorts to fear of the unknown and it is relentless in its effort to maintain control of the identity it has developed. It is the activity of the mind that drowns out the intuitive voice.

Mind activity needs reason that makes sense in three-dimensional terms and the analytical processes it has developed for finding *reason* or it falls back to its safety zone of fear or other emotional states to talk us out of the intuitive insight. Analysis and decision making are the requirements of the mind before action is taken, whereas *will* is what is needed when the intuitive insight comes. Will is what is needed because it is difficult to act in any circumstance when we have no clue as to an outcome, yet that is the nature of intuition. Some would say it takes faith, but even faith implies the essence of knowing three-dimensionally. Will does not care. It acts with the certainty that any outcome is possible but good nonetheless. Will does not even consider an outcome. *It acts!* It acts with the certainty that the intuitive voice has spoken and will let events unfold as they will. In three-dimension terms this is a truly scary thing to do! No wonder the mind is so squeamish about relinquishing control. This is the difference between thinking and intuition. Mind is tied mechanically and emotionally to caring. It cares about outcomes and looks for a *how* to everything before it moves forward with an action. Intuition detaches itself from mind and acts out of will because it has no need of caring. It moves forward with purpose without ever looking back or analyzing what could have or should have happened. Because it never judges outcomes as good or bad, it never fails; in never failing, it never loses energy to the idea of failure. When we care about outcomes, we wind ourselves up in the idea of success which is nothing more than a construct of the mind. Caring confronts us with the idea of failure and so instead of investing all of our energy in the activity at hand, we also give away our energy to *the idea of failing*. With *will*, there is no failing and consequently no loss of energy to probabilities that are nothing more than figments of our minds. Caring stresses over *supposed* future outcomes that take us out of present time. Will is always operating in present time. *Will perceives no outcomes!*

This single idea of *will* versus *caring* is perhaps the greatest barrier we face in realizing our own divine nature. The conditioning of three-dimensional life and the reality of our illusion about life is deeply rooted within each of us. To break free of it will be the most daunting thing we do, but it must be done in order to find the voice of God within. I use the word "insight" a lot when speaking about the intuitive voice because the intuitive voice is literally *inner sight*. Inner knowing comes from seeing inwardly or *insight* and recognizing that all rolled up in this thing we identify as *our self* is *the kingdom of God!* Intuition should be the loudest and only voice we hear when important matters are in play. The language of God is intuition; therefore, we all should relearn to understand and speak it. It is the only way we will know the inner workings of that God within, which we all are.

Chapter 17

Impeccability

In his book *A Separate Reality*, Carlos Castaneda's mentor Don Juan introduces us to the idea that "seeing is for impeccable men." The seeing Don Juan mentions is not the seeing we take for granted with our physical eyes. It is something much deeper that opens us up to the wondrousness of life and new levels of awareness incomprehensible in our normal three-dimensional world. It might be described as the perception of another world that is not visible in front of our eyes but only from behind the eyes. It is the knowing of the not known. It is the awareness I have spoken of previously, that while eluding our larger physical senses, it does not evade greater sensing at a cellular, if not atomic, level. We are all receptors of far more information than our three-dimensional reality comprehends, but as Don Juan asserts, it takes a certain kind of individual to see everything else that goes on around us. He uses the word "impeccable" in describing the kind of individual, a warrior or *man of knowledge* should attain in order to rise above life as we know it and become aware of wonders far greater than our current reality allows or comprehends. In using the word "impeccable," however, Don Juan never really provides a conceptual definition of what he means or what we must do to become *impeccable*, so we are left somewhat unsure. Yet, as Don Juan describes the nature of a warrior or *man of knowledge*, we can discern that such a man is able to perform incredible things not unlike the miracles of Jesus in the New Testament.

One definition of "impeccable" is "not being capable of sinning." While most Christians think of Jesus as the only *sinless* man to walk the earth, *impeccable* might mean someone like Jesus who was, as described, "without sin." Again, our illusion of reality is that we exist in a world where a demarcation between good and evil is a part of that reality. We often say that Jesus was without sin, yet there were many in his day who accused him of violation of the laws of God. To them, he was a sinner, even though most Christians would disagree. In truth, Jesus was without sin, but so too are we! There is no sin except for that to which we have been conditioned to believe. Sin is an invention of this reality and because we have accepted the criteria for this reality, we accept that sin exists in the world. As mentioned earlier, there is no sin. The idea of sin is an egotistical device to keep us questioning our value and judging our place in the world.

The dictionary definition is correct, but only in the context that we acknowledge that there is no sin in the world. It is a difficult idea to accept, but allowing it is perhaps the biggest hurdle to overcome in accepting our own impeccability. Most of us find it difficult to understand that we are without sin, as our conditioning has, over and over again, convinced us that we all do wrong things in our lives for which we will be judged. This conditioning keeps us locked in the reality we are a part of and supports our ideas that we cannot possibly be without sin.

If we look at Jesus, or even Don Juan, most would agree that they were impeccable and befitting a definition of "not being capable of sin." They were impeccable but only because they grasped the concept that there is no sin. Those who believe they sin labor over their so-called sins and indulge in deceit, regret, sorrow, and any number of emotional responses or physical acts because they believe that a normal response to being caught in sin is to hide or deny it in some way. This response, however, is due to the idea we have been conditioned to believe that any number of our actions or thoughts constitute sin. They do not, but because we cannot seem to let go of the idea that we are sinners, we have become adept at circumventing those things we say are sinful. In other words, our acceptance of the idea that we sin is the reason for trying not to get caught sinning, and so we weave ever greater webs of deceit and dishonesty so others cannot accuse us. It's as if our avoidance of sin causes more sin. This is so because the illusion of life we are a part of identifies what is sinful and how we should collectively respond to it. The responses to so-called sinning bring shame and dishonor to those caught in such acts to the extent that avoidance of being caught is the desirable alternative. Egotistically, we have tried to lessen the shame or embarrassment that comes with such identified acts by saying such things as "It's okay to make mistakes as long as you admit them." We all know that is not the case! Ultimately no one wants to be judged for his acts and condemned as a sinner. Is it any wonder that so many hide their acts to avoid such scrutiny and condemnation?

Acceptance of the idea that there is no sin is what frees us from the artificial boundaries we put around ourselves by saying that we do sin. In a state of impeccability, we are not capable of sinning because there is nothing we can do in this life or any other that constitutes such a condition. The impeccable person accepts all possibilities and all outcomes and takes responsibility for them in every way. The impeccable life has risen above the idea that we are sinners and are judged by the so-called laws of God. The impeccable life has risen above the laws of man, competition, and limitations of every kind. It is not that laws of society don't continue to exist in the world of egocentric reality, but rather we are in need of no such laws! We live in the world of others who cannot escape the illusion of our current reality, but the rules and laws imposed by a collective identity have no place in our lives. We are above them.

They are not binding on us even though we exist among those who have not escaped the illusion. In fact, even physical laws cannot hold us as he who is not capable of sin is also not bound by the laws of this three-dimensional reality.

Perhaps the most remarkable miracles Jesus performed were walking on water, stilling the storm, and raising Lazarus, his friend, from the dead. These acts were more than a demonstration of the godlike nature and power he understood and practiced; they were a demonstration of his impeccability. In other words, he was not strapped to the various conditions and ideas that everyone else had accepted as their reality. The laws of man or nature had no power over him in anyway because of his impeccable character, one that could only see himself as divine. In accepting this, he transcended all the limitations our illusions and three-dimensional reality force us into allowing.

While we can't understand or explain the things Jesus was able to do, in being impeccable, he was not bound to anything in this physical existence we hold to be true and absolute. Not only was he not bound to the laws of this three-dimensional reality, but he was also aware of so much more going on around him that most of us never see or comprehend. Impeccability is the way to awareness our limited view cannot comprehend. Impeccability is not above sinfulness, but rather *sinlessness*.

Impeccability is a state of being that sees beyond limitation imposed by any reality. It has no rules. It is purity of existence that has no boundary but encroaches on no one or thing. The impeccable life lives by will and removes itself from the so-called cares of the world. In fact, impeccability is not about caring as we know it. Caring attaches us to the world and to others in emotional ways that cause us to lose clarity of focus for those things that lie outside normal perception, causing a dimming of the awareness of all things possible by being impeccable. Impeccability is freedom from emotion and all the things we weigh ourselves down with that impede our ability to sense beyond physical sensing. Jesus taught a message that called on everyone individually to be impeccable and in so doing, all that Jesus did, including walking on water, raising the dead, commanding the elements to be still, healing the sick, and all the other things he is said to have done, would be possible for us as well. In fact, he said even greater things we could do. Impeccability is a different kind of knowing that results from a higher level of awareness that is not explainable in terms that we can adequately define. We all understand what is meant when we say "not capable of sin," but only because we have an idea of what we think is sin. When we begin to comprehend that any concept of sin is a construct of the egotistical mind, the definition of "impeccable" no longer has any meaning, and yet Don Juan had a definite impression of what he meant when he used the term. I believe he meant that being impeccable was to rise above any need for laws, either man-made or physical, so ultimately those laws would have no hold on us. This is difficult to comprehend because we are so fixed on the idea that we certainly cannot escape physical laws. But the only reason we believe this is that our conditioning has taught us this is so. So just what does it mean when Jesus announced that "All things are possible to him that believeth"? Is it just those things that our reality says is possible, or is it truly all things imaginable?

Becoming impeccable means changing our conditioning from what we know about this reality to what we don't know about it. It is accepting the idea that we are very limited in our view of how things really are and, in overcoming that limitation, we open ourselves up to the so-called impossible. Literally, we rise above law and limitation.

If Jesus had command of all the things we say he did, including the ability to bring back the living from death, why did he allow himself to be crucified? The scriptures and Christians would have us believe that he was the ultimate sacrifice for our sinfulness and that he was the price that had to be paid, the ransom as it were, for the sins of man, including the initial sin of Adam. Jesus was not a sacrifice, nor was he the ransom for our lowly and sinful nature. For Jesus to have given himself up for such an idea is inconsistent with his own teachings, that within each of us is the kingdom of God. Why establish that within each of us is the kingdom of God if no God is going to dwell there? In truth, Jesus proclaimed that the God who dwells within that kingdom, each of us has within is *us*! We are the god of that kingdom within. The treasures we seek outside will only be found inside when we uncover our own kingdom of God. Jesus knew this about himself, as he had discovered it and taught it to us so that like him, we could all experience the greater knowing and awareness he came upon in his own life. Indeed, his was an impeccable life but it was not an impossible life *for us*. He knew that all of us would have to overcome the conditioning we all undergo from birth and throughout our lives in order to find what he found, but never once did he suggest it could not be done. He was adamant that it could be done. It would require, however, recognition of our conditioning and another kind of acceptance to find our own kingdom of God within.

Jesus' death was not a sacrifice for the abstract ideas that there is sin in the world, that we are sinners, and that a perfect life must be forfeited to wipe such sins away. Jesus' death was the ultimate lesson for all of us to witness that as gods, we have power over everything we fear in life, even the ultimate fear of death. It was the final lesson given to an unbelieving world. We often hear the question that if Jesus had power over death, then why did he die? The answer is that he didn't die!! Sure, his body was nailed to the cross and physically his body "gave up the ghost," but Jesus as God, as the ultimate incarnation of what we are capable of, did not die!! His crucifixion and subsequent resurrection represented the final demonstration of the divine nature of gods, even every one of us, if we only accept our divinity as he did. Any form of death he could have been subjected to in this reality had no power over him. The critical demonstration of his power over death was to let his body die and lie in the tomb for three days so that all would be convinced he was indeed dead. He allowed enough time to elapse so that even his own disciples would begin to fall back to their old patterns of thinking that we are not gods, but lowly, sinful beings who need a savior, but alas, Jesus was not him!

Jesus did not lay down his life for our sins. *He laid down his life for our lives!!* Everything about him was a demonstration of the godlike nature and abilities we all possess. Who does not wonder about the power to take back that which is believed to be lost and what is the greatest loss we all fear? Perhaps it is the fear of death but that is only because ego has placed the question before us that after death nothing is left. We end and that is all there is. Ego fears this because the egotistical drive to find answers through science and religion cannot unequivocally know that life continues and that our essence is infinite. Ego is locked in three-dimensional reality and it fears and trembles at the "unknowns" of that reality.

Jesus' greatest miracle was not taking back his own physical life, or raising Lazarus from the dead, or walking on water, or any one of the other miracles with which he is credited. His greatest miracle was simply knowing that he was God! He knew that in such knowing, his acts, the so-called miracles he performed, were the natural outcome of knowing he was God. *Gods do what gods do!* Jesus took back his own life in a demonstration of what gods do. He did not give us back our lives or save us from eternal damnation as so many believe. He didn't need to. We can do that for ourselves since his demonstrations of power were no greater than anything we are capable of ourselves! This is what he told us.

Impeccability is being above any laws that outlines how we should be or act as individuals or as collectives of individuals. Remember it was such laws that led the collective to seek Jesus' death even though he was found by the Roman governor to have no fault. Even to the leaders of the Jews at that time, he was found to be so good or his powers were considered so great that everyone was going to believe him and it was going to disrupt the tidy little world they had established with the Roman Empire. They feared his greatness because nothing in that world they had established through time had prepared them for the things Jesus brought to it. Everything he did exceeded all their comprehension! "My ways are not your ways, neither are my thoughts your thoughts!"

Being above or greater than the laws of man is the life Jesus demonstrated and it is the essence of what Don Juan spoke of when he states that seeing is for impeccable men. Impeccable men truly are above any idea of sin and live so far beyond anything we can comprehend that we consider them strange, possessed, or mentally unbalanced. The nature of our illusional reality is to weed out those who do not fit into our perceptual and egotistical formulation of reality which we have come to accept as all there is. What we cannot understand, we must hide away because it disrupts the balance of what we think we have, just as in the days of Jesus. The leaders of the Jews in Jesus' time were not evil! They only did what they thought was necessary to maintain the balance of their conditioned reality at that time. Jesus did not condemn them. He forgave them for they "knew not what they were doing!" How could they? They were living their illusion, as we all tend to do, while Jesus lived above it! They saw him as outside their laws and constructs and could only come to the conclusion that he had to go! We all do the same in our own illusions. We accuse and judge those we do not understand and we take security in our collectives believing that what we have done was for the good of what we know to be true and for everyone who believes as we do. We do this when we judge something or someone as good or evil! How often do we label someone as weird, crazy, idiotic, or stupid when what they say or do does not align with our own sense of right or wrong? We all do this!

Jesus was in their world but not of it as he instructed all of us to do if we were to be like him. In the same way that Jesus taught us to be in the world but not of it, Don Juan termed such behavior as "controlling our folly." Controlling folly for Don Juan was a way of blending into society and living life knowing that the reality others accept for themselves, individually and societally, is not even close to what is really going on. Having greater awareness does not exclude you from the laws, institutions, and outcomes of this reality, but in that awareness, our knowing expands beyond anything this reality contains and overcomes all things imposed by that reality. Greater awareness means greater acceptance, as underscored by Jesus' words, "Forgive them for they know not what they do." In this greater awareness comes greater control over the outcomes of any reality. Very few Christians do not believe that Jesus was capable of anything he wanted, even to the extent that he could have prevented his own crucifixion or could have called legions of angels to defeat the Roman soldiers or any manner of scenarios he chose. Jesus never intended to show such possibilities because he understood that to do for others in such a way would require an egocentric mindset that he simply did not have. He would have had to conform to an attitude that "I" must help these people because they cannot help themselves. Many continue to ask why Jesus did not do more in this plane of reality that we might see as an act of greater caring such as defeating the Romans or establishing himself king like David or Solomon.

To be not of this world requires that all egotistical constructs or possibilities be cast aside. To be in the world but not of it is to give the appearance that you care about it even though you do not. You are above the reality and caring, but walk amidst the illusion as if you did. To raise oneself to the position of king or even savior, as many believe he was, requires an ego that concludes it is greater than those it will rule over, or at least fulfills the requirements to be a ruler or savior in general. You cannot be "of the world" and have anything that looks like an ego. You can, however, be impeccable and hold a place within the world of egos and live in a way that your non-egocentric life opens wonders to you beyond description. Impeccability truly is being not capable of sin but not because there is any sin. It is because the impeccable person rises above all known laws and rules and ceases to judge any act, any cause, or anyone ever again. It is the full acceptance of all aspects of life.

In introducing the idea of impeccability, Don Juan makes Carlos Castaneda and all of us aware of what such a life will become. His words are: "Temper your spirit now, become a warrior, learn to see and then you'll know that there is no end to the new worlds for our vision."

There are "new worlds" right here, right now, right in front of us! Impeccability lifts the veil drawn over us by our life of conditioning, and lets us peer out at an infinite, incomprehensible reality that will leave us breathless in its wake! Impeccability is not about being incapable of sin. It is about being infinitely capable!

Chapter 18

The Real Mystery

The great mysteries of life should exist outside our inner selves, but they don't. Instead the greatest mystery in life has become the ever elusive quest to find the inner self. Our own inner selves have become so lost in the illusion of exterior life that inner knowing is now the great *unknown*.

What we perceive through our physical senses should be the greatest mystery of life and yet we have focused so much attention on *what is out there* that we think we have come to know it in a familiar way and that somehow all the unanswered questions that well up from the very foundation of our souls will be answered there. We praise science for showing us so much and for explaining how the universe works. With the technologies that have come from such exploration, our lives have become simplified and comfortable; the knowledge of so much is at our very fingertips. Our industry and productivity is like nothing ever before experienced in all of human kind. Our knowledge base increases to levels never thought possible a few short years ago. We are all so much a part of this vast reality that gives so much to man that we look only to it for answers to all of life's questions. Even the deeper questions that come from within and never seem to be satisfied with the answers the outer existence provides.

However, in this reality of knowing all that we know, our inner selves have been pushed aside and while we are caught up in something wonderful and mysterious on the outside, we are lost on the inside. So lost are we to any true meaning of self, the inner god we all are has become the *real* mystery in life where there should be no such mystery. In other words, the *perceptive ego* has become obsessed with finding and keeping itself safe in the world without and in so doing, has kept hidden from us what we really are. The focus of science is directed ever outward into the smallest of things or the largest of things in its effort to understand how everything came to be and asks it's questions in the same manner as any religious institution would, specifically looking outward to God and asking for answers to how He thinks. Scientific experts ask, "Why this way or that?" or "What is He thinking?" as they look for answers to life's mysteries and religious leaders proclaim, "Show me your ways." Neither looks to the inner world of man where god really exists and explore the inner self that is divine and the *true* creative center of the universe. Religion castigates and condemns man, relegating him to a lowly and sinful state while science, looking outward to the stars or inward to the smallest particle, labels him an accident of space and time. Both speak to the miracle of man but see him as something that could only exist because of some exterior force, based somewhere out there in the heavens, that they can only describe in abstract ways.

What we really are is not and never will be found outside us and realizing that cannot happen by looking outward to a god in heaven for he is not out there. The essence of what we are is not out there somewhere in the so-called heavens as religious leaders would have us believe nor is it found through science in the inner world of quantum particles or the vastness of space. It is not in nature or things, knowledge, credentials, or anything else our thinking has determined to be so. None of these things can illuminate something they cannot possibly understand in an intellectual way. Gods do not speak the language of man; therefore, the language of man could never explain God! Even if man understood and knew completely his own inner divinity, could he find any words in human languages that could describe or explain it. It is a knowing that transcends language. It is a knowing that transcends three-dimensional, physical sensing.

What we are resides within us. Who we are is only identifiable from within. This should not be a mystery, but it is. We have created a world that continuously strives to identify with *things* outside ourselves whether it be physical objects such as cars, homes, toys, etc., or affiliations such as religion, politics, race, or ideas. Without such identifiable qualifiers, we are completely lost and frustrated when those things fail to provide us the security, comfort, or identity we so desperately seek. Identification with anything "out there" will always fail because *we are not that which we have projected to the world outside ourselves.* All of us know this on some level, but the illusion of the world we have created has led us to look ever outward for answers to everything!

The greatest mysteries in life should be the world and the universe outside of ourselves. What we have created instead makes that world outside a place of safety and identity and *the world within has become the mystery when it should be our greatest knowing!* Most of us search desperately outside for anything that might give us inner clarity and help us to comprehend our true selves but rarely find it. While we are awed by the beauty of the earth and the magnificence of our inventions, creations, and knowledge, we fear the callous nature of the reality we all seem to live in and yet it is the place we go to find deep inner knowing. We ask anyone but ourselves for the answers to these deeply rooted questions that are so mysterious to us. Why is inner knowing such a mystery when it should be our greatest source of comfort and peace regardless of where we are looking in the outer world? *Out there* should be a mystery, not *in here!* Our identity of *out there* is why we become afraid, feel pain, sorrow, and suffering. The development or discovery of our inner selves, our soul as it were, is where we overcome fears, pain, and suffering. Nothing out there can have any effect on us if we find that inner self, that god within that is greater than anything our physical reality can throw at us. Yet we continue to search outside for that knowing which is only found inside. The *I Am* within should not be a mystery to any of us; most of us, however, could not describe ourselves to anyone else without using egotistical terms, credentials, or identifiers that are so common in our language today. These elements of our language connect us again and again to the world outside, to the illusion we have accepted about ourselves, and to our fellow humans.

It is mysterious and wondrous out *there*, but it cannot be comprehended nor can we overcome any fear of it unless we find who we are inside. We have the power right now to find everything we seek, *out there*, within us. We are after all gods who are made up of infinite power and have command of such power at all times. It is not *out there* somewhere. It is in us right now, infinite and untapped.

We possess all things we claim God to be right now in our own selves, and yet the prevailing scientific and religious beliefs lead us away from this knowing into a false sense of security that something *out there* will take care of us. This sense of security permeates every aspect of our lives from our jobs to our health to retirement, happiness, and so on. Our searching for the god without has conditioned us that somehow, some way, something out there is going to provide for our every need. We look to our governments, our companies, and other outside entities to support us and help us through difficult times believing that they have the means and ability to do it. There is nothing out there that is going to take care of us. *We* are all we've got! All strength and power to command the life we want comes from within. Inner knowing knows no fear and thus is all-powerful in our walk through life with the full knowledge that nothing can harm us and that all our needs will be taken care of. We can control our lives and never be without the assurance that from inward knowing we have always been, are, and will always be all-powerful. We need to re-learn that. Actually, we need to remember that. We need to remember what we knew at birth but forgot as we were systematically re-taught otherwise.

We were born with everything we needed to create a wonderful and plentiful world. We came with knowledge that the greatest of our greatest thinkers could not comprehend, but it became veiled by the ideas and knowing those thinkers contribute to and support. We all know on some level our universal or infinite nature. Some call it 'divine' but we all know we are part of something too incredible and wondrous to comprehend in any scientific or religious way. We are all of this and more. We are shining lights that burn with endless power and infinite brightness. *And we burn forever!*

Recent theories in chaos have determined that small, seemingly insignificant, perturbations of conditions can cause huge changes to the overall system. It is sometimes referred to as the butterfly effect. The mind of man can theorize that a butterfly fluttering its wings in Africa can cause a hurricane to alter its course so that it hits landfall in Florida when it was originally destined to peter out somewhere in the Atlantic ocean. Surely the mind of God can create the ocean that the hurricane forms in or the earth where that ocean resides. The inner mind of man *is* the mind of God. The inner mind of man is the center, the creative center of the universe. The inner mind of man is the *divine, the god, we seek, the answer to all our questions the provider of all things!*

It is not the identifiable things we sense in our reality that gives us identity. Those things, even all things we have allowed to be, because of the illusion of what we now call life, have been learned throughout a lifetime. Those things are only real in terms of how we perceive them, based on that learning that comes from the illusion we are all part of! Everything we see through physical senses or have come to believe is so much greater than that seeing or believing could possibly comprehend, *and so are we!*

We need to unlearn everything we have been taught about the objective world in order to see beyond what we have learned it is. Our reality is an interpretation we make by ourselves because that is how we have been conditioned to see it. It doesn't need to be what we have come to believe it is. We can change it anytime to virtually anything we want, but more importantly, we can see beyond it to *what really is!!* Gods have that power.

Unlearning is a hard thing to do, especially when all of our learning gets tied to the identity of who we are. Most of us live our lives in story form. In other words, we see ourselves and even refer to ourselves as the culmination of our historical actions and accomplishments, whatever they may be, and call that history *what* or *who* we are. We also consist of dreams and aspirations for the future and the doubts and fears raised in those dreams.

We pick up a lot of junk on the journey that gets connected to us as well. In fact, most, if not all, of it is junk in the sense that it contributes nothing to the present moment or life. It is only *content* that gives substantiation to our particular story, our reality. Whether we label our story 'good' or 'bad,' it is full of historical junk that serves only to keep the story of us alive. All history, be it personal or social, is biased because it is always told from someone's perspective. Put another way it is a one-sided perspective remembered and told to uphold our own perception of reality. It is not a true story since we can never know all sides of it, yet the story we hold, holds us. We are not its product; *we are its victim.* We are fictional characters in a fictional story that builds inexorably "Line upon line and precept upon precept." That fiction becomes rigid and finite and we are trapped in it of our own making. We have accepted our place in the complex story of man that plays out before us everyday. Our history ties us to it and with each passing day, the illusion becomes more complex and our place within it becomes more fixed.

Those who shed their story, their history, are free of the *stuff* of life. They are free of the historical baggage that carries forward and factors into every aspect of their present lives. They are free of roles such as mother, father, child, good son, bad daughter, good neighbor, bad neighbor, and so on. They are free of the rules and expectations that are given to those roles. They are free of the fictional illusions that weave themselves into the fabric of everyday life and living. Shedding historical junk frees us from fears and anxiety built up over our lives that tie us to all our viewpoints, judgments, and arguments, comprising the reality we think of as what or who we are.

Typically what we have come to accept as what we are becomes the substance of what ego must now protect and uphold. It doesn't matter if it is seen as good or bad. It is now the stuff of our own self *importance* and self importance is what fuels our negative emotions. Self importance is the sinister judge we create within ourselves that must compare every act, every condition, and every event to its own set of standards and rate the lives and actions of others according to them. All of our emotions arise out of this so called "breaking of the rules." Fear, anger, jealousy, sadness, and doubt drain us of energy but our historical illusions must be upheld when ego has taken hold of them. The story must be maintained and reinforced; so now our low-level emotions, fueled by an ever burgeoning story, become the direction of our creative power. In other words, the way we are as derived from that story – the junk of the past – our history, feeds the very creative process that could be used to greater ends, greater understanding, and greater awareness! We literally bring into our lives more circumstances, more situations, more people and things that cause the story to grow.

We have such power and if your life is moving in a way that is unsatisfactory to you, look at your story. Look at the junk in your closet that you have attached energy to. The energy that is consumed by maintaining a story, or a fragment of a story, is energy that cannot be used toward more gainful purposes. It is also energy, however, that is attracting like energy. It resonates and draws to it people, places, events, and things that vibrate at the same frequency. This is how it continues to find itself, to grow, and to empower itself.

Our story, whatever it is, is the reference point for whatever comes into our lives. The bigger the story, the greater the amount of junk stored that supports that story, and the greater the attractive power to invoke similar circumstances that resonate with that story. Coupled with that ever increasing story is the greater amount of energy consumed along the way.

In truth, our history is of no consequence to anyone but ourselves and yet we hang on to it as if everyone in the world should care. *Ego identity is historical identity.* Ego will think and talk endlessly about how it came to be by recounting traumas, education, credentials, travels, and accomplishments that it presumes important to everyone else! *Everyone out there!* Again, everything ego does pushes its way outward for others to see. *Outward* is where the ego directs its focus.

Sadly, the story becomes so consuming that we lose ourselves in it to the extent we cannot see anything outside it. Some will resort to platitudes such as "That's the hand I was dealt," or "This is what my life was meant to be," etc. Many who read these words will not comprehend that outside of their wishing for something better, their story, which has such an insidious grip on their lives and requires a great deal of energy to maintain, is pulling more and more things to them that supports the conditions and circumstances they find themselves in. Some, perhaps most, never get out of it as it becomes a vicious circle that never ends and ever grows.

This is the basis for the idea that "life just happens" which is the case for most people.

Most people don't know why so many negative and unpleasant things happen to them and they are indignant that anyone would accuse them of *attracting* such things in their lives. Who wouldn't be indignant at such an accusation? Ego knows better than to overtly make such claims, but ego also knows better than anyone what story lies at the core of every individual, and it is the resonant frequency of that story that calls forth the things we gather to us, be they good or bad. How we perceive it makes no difference. How we resonate is the way our life will go. What we resonate is what we attract. At the core of resonance is a story, a historical perspective, *the egotistical fuel of our experience.* It is the make up of our being.

This is why it is so difficult to turn around and why so many people fail to enjoy the things they dream about. The frequency of your vibration *is* the life you live. It is the life your inherent nature creates. It is not enough to change what you say and do. Most of what you say and do is the outward appearance of what your ego wants to show to the world. Most of what we manifest outwardly is the illusion we want to project to others, thus adding to the fiction that is playing out every day. You must change who you are at a deeply inner level, one that most do not want to face or admit exists. Ego fears this and works diligently to fend off these kinds of onslaughts. It has gone to great effort to project a different image to the world and heaven forbid you change it! You must change the story of your life or eliminate it altogether. In either case, the new story must use less energy than the old, while eliminating the story preserves all the energy once used to uphold and feed the story.

Changing who you are is difficult because it requires that you alter or eliminate your story. Changing your story is difficult because it is what gets tied up with ego, and ego, *clever beast* that it is, the very thing it has come to identify *you* with the world, will not let go without a fight. It won't let go easily, yet it must be done.

How is it done? How do we change our story? For some, giving up their stories comes suddenly and profoundly. It may happen as a result of a traumatic event or near-death experience in which the very foundation of their souls is shaken in such a way that nothing preceding that event matters anymore. It is almost as if the previously held story was radically removed in an invasive way such as cutting out a tumor from the physical body. It's hard to explain how this happens, but people who have experienced such removal are forever changed and different from that point on. The newness and calm of their lives is physically detectable. Nothing seems to matter, or certainly not in the ways it did before. Not even the thought or prospect of death consumes their energy. Such a change might be looked at as a spiritual transformation, but regardless of what it is called, it is evident that something profound and wonderful has happened.

Some terminally ill people experience the same kind of transformation and, while fully aware of their impending mortality, they take on a sweetness and acceptance that is unexplainable to those who knew them just a short time earlier. They are simply free of the historical encumbrances that previously defined them and with nothing to show or hide, they are more than ever before completely themselves, perhaps for the first time in their lives. Many of us know of such people. Physically they look younger, their eyes twinkle and shine, and the stress they once carried in their faces dissipates.

Most of us will not go through these kinds of experiences. Most of us will have to change our story a piece at a time. Changing one's story does not imply making up something new to replace what we believe actually happened. It is more a process of re-evaluating events in our lives that continue to draw our energy. For instance, most childhood memories are benign and innocent and we can look back on them with a fondness that makes us smile or laugh. There are, however, events and circumstances that we continue to carry with us which shape us and our outcomes throughout our lives. Most often these events involved interactions of some kind with other humans, be they parents, siblings, relatives, teachers, etc. These may include experiences such as embarrassments, infringements, friendships, confrontations with perhaps school bullies, rivalries, punishments, mental and emotional abuses, and on and on. We probably don't think of these *events* or *people* anymore, but we all react to certain situations or circumstances in a way where the punishment does not meet the crime. Ego has no need for specific memory as long as it can harbor the raw emotion the original event raised in us.

All of the past events of which I am speaking are often looked at philosophically and we think they are inconsequential. However, the trauma and emotion they carried with them at the time are typically what stays with us and hidden from any conscious view. Additionally, what we are taught to believe hardens our perception and locks us into "the way it is," preventing the exploration of anything outside or beyond that view. Even while acknowledging that there is something greater than what we perceive, we defend our perception with rigid certainty.

The description of the world we perceive is the filter through which we analyze everything, making it even more difficult to see beyond what we see. If something, a belief or idea or thought, settles on us out of the blue, ego instantly grabs it and squeezes it through that filter. If it passes through, whatever that filter consists of, it is allowed and added to the depository of other thoughts and ideas that make us who we are. If it does not pass through it, is sliced, diced, and thrown out, never having the opportunity to enlighten us.

Yes, we are what we think about, but we shouldn't be. The saying might be better stated "We are what we are." Our thinking is limited, finite. What we *are* is not. We are infinite and the only way we can ever know that is to stop our thinking and prevent our egocentric natures from convincing us of the finiteness of life and everything else.

The mystery of life should not be *who we are!* It should be no mystery that we are greater than anything our thinking can produce or anything our ego considers defensible. There is wonder and beauty in everything and *what we truly are,* our divine natures, know this! *What we think* does not. What we truly are knows no bounds and is open in every way to everything that happens whether it is judged 'good' or 'evil' by thinking, finite man.

What we are knows no duality. There is no good or evil, nor choices between a so-called right or wrong. There are no choices of any kind since no choice is a bad or good choice. Life simply flows onward and with each moment that we get to experience it in all its variety and beauty, it is a gift, an enhancement, to who we are and to the awareness we develop through that living.

The gift of life is awareness. It is an awareness that recognizes there are no mysteries that cannot be comprehended at the deep inner level that comes with knowing our divine nature. True awareness only exists in knowing the divine self, the *I Am,* and then, in *being who we are!* Awareness comes to those who look at everything in existence without judgments of any kind and accept all outcomes as neither good nor bad but only a part of the infinite stream of life. Such knowing can only come from within. From this inner knowing, that with all things, we too are a part of a stream of life and that whatever course it takes, we are a part of it as it is with us. Such mysteries will never be understood or comprehended by the thinking mind. Life lived through the filter of thinking and egocentric constructs is a limited life. It is a finite life, one of ever looking outward for that which can only be found inward. It is not possible to know God, your inner self, intellectually, however, if you should find and come to know that divine inner self that you are, it will not be possible to describe it intellectually either. It knows not the language of humans and will not speak to you in those terms.

The change of awareness from our current illusion can only be known at some deep inner level that has no explanation in the present reality. Our language will never be able to adequately describe such a knowing. You will simply know and it will be so deeply understood that it will change your awareness of everything in existence. There will be no need for explanation in any language. God does not speak the language of man, but does speak to the soul of man. The language of the soul knows all and that will be enough. That *is* the voice of God.

Are we the life we live or are we the life we *think* we live? There is only one person in existence who knows this. YOU! Only you can look inward and find your divine nature, your God, and have power come forth that is greater than all the creative power of the universe.

Do not live the life you think you know. Be the life you are!!

For further information contact:

http://www.onbeinggod.com

Carl's official website